makes for
mini folk

lisa stickley

PAVILION

for mum and dad

First published in the United Kingdom in 2018 by
Pavilion
43 Great Ormond Street
London
WC1N 3HZ

Distributed in the United States and Canada by
Sterling Publishing Co, Inc.
1166 Avenue of the Americas
New York, NY 10036

ISBN 978-1-911595-43-4

A CIP catalogue record for this book is available from the British Library.

10 9 8 7 6 5 4 3 2 1

Reproduction by Mission Productions, Hong Kong
Printed and bound by Toppan Leefung Printing Ltd, China

This book can be ordered direct from the publisher at www.pavilionbooks.com

PAVILION

Whatever the craft, we have the book for you – just head straight to Pavilion's crafty headquarters.

Pavilion Craft is the one-stop destination for all our fabulous craft books. Sign up for our regular newsletters and follow us on social media to receive updates on new books, competitions and interviews with our bestselling authors.

We look forward to meeting you!

www.pavilionbooks.com/craft

easy as a, b, c

to the big folk

I've been a maker since the early '80s (I was VERY little then), and a mother since 2014. Having mini ones turns your world upside down and gives you a WHOLE new perspective on life. Seeing things through the untainted, energetic and super enthusiastic eyes of a little person is such a refreshing experience. And the inspiration they bring is immense.

Whether you're a mum, dad, auntie, uncle, grandparent or friend, hopefully this book will inspire you to make some mini bits for the mini folk in your life. Yes, there are many, many great things you can buy from the shops for the arrival of a new being. But how much nicer to give something you have actually made; a super special piece that will be loved, well worn and potentially passed on in its affectionately adored and slightly squiffy state.

I love being a mum and love making things, both for my minis and with them. Throughout the chapters there are practical pieces, quirky items, essential bits, super fun things and even grand projects. There are easy-peasy items of clothing and, personally, once I started, I haven't been able to stop making fun, colourful and one-size-fits-many outfits for my two minis. Particularly the overalls, which I might have to scale up to adult size one day soon!

In the months before babies arrive, time is quite different to the rather limited time you have once they've 'popped out'. If you're a maker like me, embracing a project when you're waddling about like a beached whale is a fantastic distraction from all of that pensive waiting. Once you are through the first few frantic months post-birth, a simple project here and there is a welcome break.

So many people I meet find the process of making extremely restorative and refreshing. Just as a good walk can 'air the brain', making also seems to have that recharging effect.

Each chapter contains a mix of projects, from easy ones that can be whipped up during nap time, through to some slightly more complicated ones to challenge the mind just a little bit. I've also added 'Mini Makes' in-between each chapter to inspire you to do some fun stuff with the kids too!

For me, to reuse and recycle is a wondrous thing – lots of the projects in this book call for bits and pieces you might have hanging around: an old worn-out pillow case you can shred and use for stuffing; small scraps of patterned fabrics you don't want to throw away but just don't know what to do with; corrugated cardboard packaging you'd usually send for recycling that can be cut, painted and turned into something super fun! It makes things a little easier on the pocket too, as, let's face it, minis cost money!

I've included a good mix of techniques: appliqué, transfer printing, 'colouring-in' with fabric dye sticks, 'poppering' with snap pliers (my new obsession), and combining digitally printed illustrations with simple embroidery, to give real individuality to items. In terms of sewing, lots of the projects use a simple straight stitch, with the most complicated challenges being stitching a buttonhole or fitting a zip. So, even if you are just a beginner on the sewing machine, there are plenty of projects that aren't too tricky.

I've LOVED making this book. It has been great to get back on the sewing machine and into my 'mini workshop/den' in a big way. I wanted to make a book full of makes for mini folk that also reflected the doodles and illustrations from my children's books, and I think maybe they do. We quite like them in our house – I really hope you like them and enjoy making them too!

Lisa x

basics and techniques

handy tools and materials

Good tools will make your life a lot easier when making and doing, especially when you have limited time. Here are the basics you will need and a few extras too.

I would just note that it will drive you completely bonkers if you don't have a decent pair of fabric scissors and new blades for your craft knife. Trying to cut fabric with crummy scissors makes me want to cry – as does cutting paper or card with fabric scissors! The cardboard projects are great fun to make, BUT if you use a blunt blade you will probably throw them out the window in frustration halfway through! Just saying.

TOOLS
- Basic sewing machine
- Zipper foot for sewing machine
- Buttonhole foot for sewing machine
- Freehand-embroidery foot for sewing machine (optional)
- Embroidery hoop (optional)
- Seam ripper/quick unpick (comes in handy for sewing mistakes!)
- Hand-sewing needles in various sizes
- Pins
- Bodkin
- Embroidery/small sharp scissors
- Large fabric scissors
- Zips
- Pencil
- Chalk
- Chalk pencil
- Safety pins
- Tape measure
- Iron and ironing board
- Hot glue gun and glue sticks
- Craft knife and blades
- Cutting mat

- Paint brushes in various sizes
- Paint (emulsion, coloured paints, chalkboard paint)
- Coloured fabric crayons
- Binder clips
- Buttons
- Snap pliers and plastic poppers/ snap fixings

MATERIALS
- Fabrics of your choice (see page 10 for more information)
- Cotton sewing thread in various colours
- Embroidery thread in various colours
- Iron-on adhesive webbing
- Interfacing
- 3mm/⅛in elastic
- Corrugated card (start collecting old boxes)
- String
- Toy stuffing

fabrics

To keep things simple, for this book I have mostly used a lighter-weight cotton poplin/sheeting for the clothing projects, and a medium-weight cotton/linen for the cushions and toys.

I have a box of vintage scraps and odds and ends of patterned fabrics, which I've collected over the years, to use for appliqué and smaller items such as the Bendable Book (p.20). Alternatively I often up-cycle old pillowcases or sheets.

For the Sleep Sack (p.37), I've recommended an organic cotton fleece for the warmer version.

I've deliberately kept the fabrics natural rather than synthetic, as I think they are much nicer for little ones. For felt, I would recommend getting a wool/polyester mix, rather than 100% synthetic, for strength and quality.

If you would like to buy digitally printed fabrics featuring my patterns and designs – which may prove particularly helpful for the Embroidered Cushion (p.34), the Lion Cushion (p.112) and the Gerald Giraffe Height Chart (p.119) – they are available to order via Woven Monkey (see p.143). Woven Monkey are set up for small, one-off projects, have good prices and deliver worldwide. From the fabric selections available, I used the cotton poplin 126gsm as the light-weight option, and the cotton/linen 228gsm for the mid-weight fabric.

You'll find details of my other favourite fabric suppliers on p.143.

tips on techniques

cutting templates from fabric
Templates for the projects can be found on pages 129–142. Lay your template flat on your fabric and pin around the edges to hold it in place. Draw around the pieces with a sharp chalk pencil, then cut around the outline with fabric scissors.

machine stitches
I mostly use a straight stitch throughout the book. At the beginning and end of all seams I recommend back-stitching a few times to secure the thread, before snipping off the loose ends. 'Topstitching' refers to a visible line of straight stitching, usually done from the right side of the fabric. Take your time with this as it will be seen on your finished project.

freehand embroidery
If you are confident on your sewing machine and would like to try freehand embroidery, a freehand-embroidery foot and embroidery hoop will come in very handy for the more 'illustrated' projects, such as the Height Chart (p.119) or the Embroidered Cushion (p.34).

Transfer the design to the fabric (see p.11), then fit your fabric into a hoop. Stretch the fabric taut in the outer hoop and push the inner hoop down on top. Use the freehand-embroidery foot on your sewing machine and go back and forth along the lines (as if colouring-in with a pencil). If you don't have a freehand-embroidery foot, go over the lines 3 or 4 times with a small, straight machine stitch using the regular foot.

transferring designs to fabric
Enlarge the embroidery design as indicated on the template using a photocopier or scanner. Tape the photocopied design onto a window, and tape your fabric on top of the photocopy. Trace the design onto your fabric using a soft pencil or a water soluble marker, to make an outline that will either be hidden by your stitching, or which is easy to remove once the embroidery is complete.

seams
A basic seam is used to join two pieces of fabric together in a single line. Place the two pieces of fabric to be joined right sides together. Pin in place. Create the seam by making a straight line of stitches, parallel to the raw edge of the fabric. I use a 1cm/½in seam allowance, unless specified otherwise. Back-stitch at the beginning and end of the seam to secure.

When stitching a curved seam, clipping curves and cutting notches makes things a great deal neater when turning out. After sewing the seam, make small regular cuts in the raw seam allowance, almost up to – but not cutting through – the seam.

For corner seams (see Lunch Bag project, p.54), it's a good idea to clip the seam allowance diagonally across the corner, to give a neat finish when turning through.

turning out and pressing
When turning out, I run my fingers along the inside of the seam, gently easing it out, and then roll the seam out from the outside with my fingers, to ensure the seam is fully turned out before pressing.

pin-tucking
In this book, pin-tucking is used for the toadstool stalk in the Bendable Book (p.20). Ideally you want it a bit wonky, so perfect pin-tucking isn't essential. The basic pin-tucking method is as follows:

Prepare your iron and ironing board, then with your fabric panel wrong side up and starting at the left-hand side, fold the edge of the fabric over by ½cm/¼in. Press. Stitch a line down the length of the fold, 3mm/⅛in from the edge. Press the seam open on the back, then turn back to the right side and press the pin tuck to the left. Measuring from the newly stitched line, repeat the ½cm/¼in fold, press and create a second line of stitches 3mm/⅛in from the folded edge. Press to the left and repeat for the width of the fabric.

buttonholes
For machined buttonholes, I recommend following the manufacturer's instructions for your particular machine, as they vary enormously depending on the model and type of foot you have.

For hand-sewn buttonholes, make a slit in the fabric in the desired position to the width of the button. With a needle and thread, secure the thread to the top of the slit and then draw the needle through the fabric from back to front, around 6mm/¼in from the raw fabric edge. Before you pull the thread taut, loop it around the needle making a knot on the raw fabric edge. Continue in this way, with closely repeated neat stitches, until you've created a secure buttonhole edging all the way around the slit.

using iron-on adhesive webbing
Make sure you stick the shiny side of the webbing to the fabric, to avoid messing up your iron. An old piece of cotton fabric comes in handy here, to lay on top of the webbing and the fabric to which you're attaching it, to protect your iron further. I find it easiest to attach webbing to fabric before cutting out shapes for appliqué.

appliqué

When you have pressed the adhesive webbing to the back of your appliqué fabric, cut to size. Remove the backing paper, position onto your main fabric and press with your iron to fix. Finally, stitch around the appliquéd piece as close to the edge as possible. This stitching is essential for permanently securing the appliquéd shape.

zips and zip-ends

For the projects that require zips, I used nylon closed-end dress zips.

A zip-end is a small rectangle of lightweight fabric, used to create a neat finish on a zip. Use a 3 x 4cm/1 x 1½in piece of cotton. Cut the zip to the desired length and position the fabric on top of the zip at the end, right sides together. Stitch a 1cm/½in seam across the width of the zip. Fold the unstitched end of the fabric over by 1cm/½in, then fold it right the way round to the back side of the zip (covering the raw edge of the zip). Machine stitch in place, making sure to catch the turned underside of the zip-end as you do. See also diagrams on p.51.

When inserting a zip, prepare the 2 panels of fabric to be fitted to the zip by pressing a 1cm/½in hem along the edge of each piece. With the zip right side up, line up the folded edge of the fabric panel, right side up, along one edge of the zip, with the folded hem tucked under. Using the zipper foot on your machine, stitch through the layers of fabric and the zip all at once. Repeat on the other side. Practice makes perfect – if it's your first time, practise with some old zips and fabric first.

using fabric dye sticks

These are fab. Hold your fabric taut and colour-in to achieve your desired effect. Lay an old piece of cloth on top of your coloured fabric before pressing with a hot iron to fix.

using snap pliers and poppers/ snap fixings

These are GREAT. I bought a set of snap pliers to use for this book and am in love! Mine came with no instructions so I looked it up on YouTube – there are a number of videos to be found online which will give you a guide. You can of course stitch a popper to a piece of fabric, but really these pliers are pretty self-explanatory.

Poppers/snap fixings come in 4 parts: 2 caps, 1 stud part and 1 socket part. Place the cap in position on the right side of your fabric and either the stud or socket on the wrong side, then line up and press with the pliers until firmly fixed together.

hot glueing

Follow the instructions for your particular glue gun. My top tips would be to get the children far away before starting, have lots of glue sticks at the ready and, after each 'squeeze', touch the end of the gun firmly to the card (or whatever you are glueing) to stop the flow of the hot glue. Speed is of the essence, especially when glueing large areas (such as the Hobby Horse, p.104). Hold the items you are glueing together for a good few minutes or, if possible, pile heavy books on top to hold in place while setting.

before you start

Use the projects in the book as starting points, but adapt them however you like. The clothing projects can be easily scaled up or down to fit a variety of shapes and sizes. They are also forgiving enough to suit growing bodies. Elastic is a godsend for mini ones and new mums alike! Hurrah for elastic!

Don't forget to follow only one set of measurements, metric or imperial, when making projects, otherwise you will get yourself in a right pickle.

'Mini Fun' makes are projects to do with your mini ones. There are some cutting and hot-glueing elements involved, so assistance and supervision from a grown up is required. Aside from those 'don't try this at home' bits for the little ones, they are good fun!

get making

I've included a quick 'from the toolbox' key at the beginning of each project. These symbols will give you a 'glance-and-grab' guide to the main tools and basic materials you'll need to complete it. You'll also find these symbols next to the step-by-step illustrations to highlight particularly handy bits and pieces to have to hand at each stage of the make.

tape measure

needle

pencil

elastic

bodkin

sewing machine

coloured fabric dye sticks

embroidery scissors

thread

craft knife

safety pin or nappy/diaper pin

pins

large fabric scissors

iron and ironing board

emulsion/ household paint

paint brushes

hot glue gun and glue sticks

string

coloured paint

binder clip

snap pliers and poppers/snap fixings

brilliant bib

This is a very easy one to make and an essential piece of kit for any new mum or dad. It can be whipped up in an hour, then you can wrap it in tissue, box up your bib and bestow on a baby!

1. Using the template on p.129, cut 1 x outer and 1 x lining piece.

Pin the 2 pieces with right sides together, and stitch all around the outside, allowing a seam. Leave a 10cm/4in gap at the base to turn out.

Clip the curves all round, turn out and press the seams flat.

from the toolbox

things you need

- Main fabric – nice printed cotton (50 x 50cm/½ x ½yd)
- Cotton lining – I used a simple ecru for this one (50 x 50cm/½ x ½yd)
- Cotton thread
- 1 x button
- Buttonhole foot for sewing machine (optional)

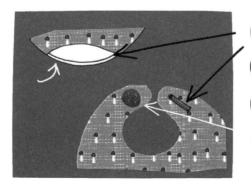

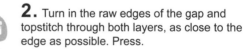

2. Turn in the raw edges of the gap and topstitch through both layers, as close to the edge as possible. Press.

Following the instructions on your sewing machine, or using the 'hand-sewn' method (see p.11), make a buttonhole to fit your button at the end of the right-hand neck flap.

Line up and stitch your button in place at the end of the neck flap.

long-legged nell

I loved making this. She takes patience to stuff, but when she's complete, just to wiggle Nell's legs about and give her a squeeze is well worth the effort. I used a vintage fabric, but a light denim or medium-weight cotton would also work well.

from the toolbox

things you need

- Body – medium-weight cotton or light denim (66cm x 1m/26 x 39in)
- 1 x bag of soft-toy stuffing (500g/1lb 2oz)
- Tail – dark-brown braid trim, or cord (12cm/4½in)
- Coloured cotton thread (including dark brown for eye)

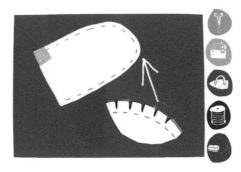

1. Using the templates on p.137, cut 2 x body pieces and 4 x ear pieces, from the body fabric.

With right sides together, pin then stitch 2 of the ear pieces together, with a ½cm/¼in seam, leaving the flat end open. Clip the curve, turn out and press. Repeat for second ear.

Turn over one end of the tail trim by ½cm/¼in, turn again by the same amount, and stitch to hem.

2. With right sides together, pin the body pieces together, placing the raw edges of the ears and tail in position as you do so (see diagram). Stitch all around the outside, allowing a ½cm/¼in seam, and leaving a 10cm/4in gap under the tail for turning out.

Get a cup of tea, a couple of cookies and a comfy chair and turn out, using a pencil to ease the seams.

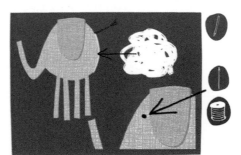

3. Now stuff. Take it bit-by-bit, stuffing fully but not too firmly, working on the legs, the trunk and finally the body.

Moving the stuffing aside a little, turn in the raw edges of the gap and whipstitch or topstitch to close, as close to the edge as possible.

Hand-embroider a small dot for the eyes on either side of the head, with lots of tiny straight stitches. Give Nell a squidge around, evenly distributing the stuffing, and that's it – another well-deserved cup of tea required!

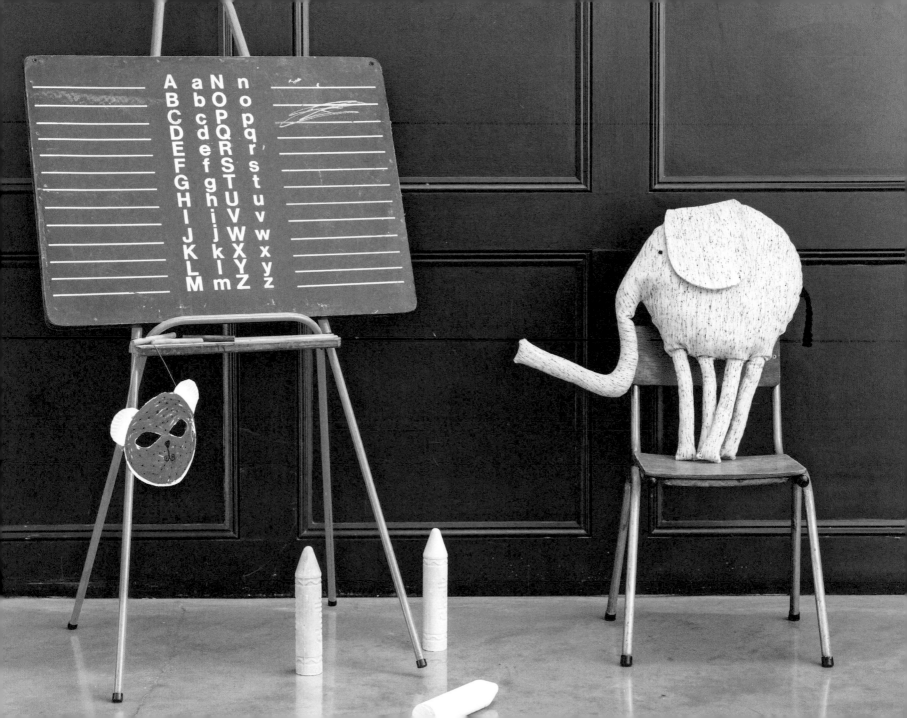

bendable book

Mini folk love to squish, rustle and fiddle with a flexible fabric book, and how nice to make your own. This isn't the fastest project, but it's not complicated – it just has a few more stages than the others. A PERFECT mum-to-be project for the long days before the mini one arrives, it's also fantabulous for anyone with a crafty twinkle in their eye to make for a new arrival.

You will make 4 double-page book spreads that are then sewn together to create an 8-page book, including covers.

spread 1

spread 2

spread 3

spread 4

things you need

- Fabric for pages – each spread is 32 x 16cm/ 12½ x 6¼in. I used a lightweight linen in ecru for 2 pages and petrol blue linen for the other 2 (a total quantity of 1 x 1.4m/39 x 55in will be just the ticket)
- Appliqué pieces – small offcuts of colourful/ patterned fabric, or plain fabrics 'coloured-in' with dye sticks (see p.12)
- Colourful felt (make sure it has some real wool content and isn't wholly synthetic)
- Cotton thread (various colours)
- String (50cm/20in)
- Scrunchy plastic (cereal packaging is good) (30 x 14cm/12 x 5½in)
- Iron-on adhesive webbing (50 x 50cm/ 20 x 20in is plenty)
- Lightweight iron-on interfacing (20 x 20cm/8 x 8in)
- 2 x large buttons (4cm/1½in in diameter)

from the toolbox

1. Cut 4 pieces of fabric for the pages to size (32 x 16cm/12½ x 6¼in). Spreads 1 and 3 are ecru coloured and Spreads 2 and 4 are petrol blue coloured.

Refer back to these diagrams (right) for reference as you are making the different elements.

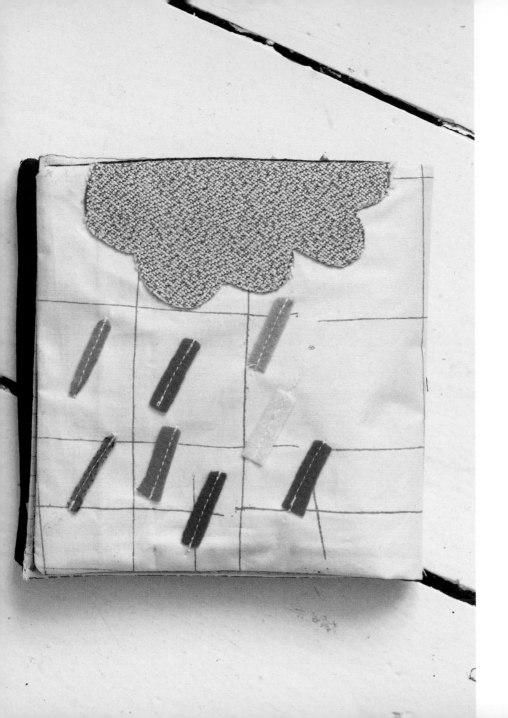

2. Prepare the first piece of ecru fabric with a freehand-drawn large criss-cross pattern, using fabric dye sticks (see p.12).

Fix the adhesive webbing on the back of your 'cloud' fabric (see p.11) and, using the template on p.139, cut out the cloud. Position the cloud at the top of the page, referring to the spread 1 diagram on p.21, and iron to fix. Topstitch all the way round to secure, stitching as close to the edge as possible.

Cut some multi-coloured raindrops from the felt pieces, using the template on p.138. Pin to position on the page and stitch each one down the centre to secure.

SPREAD 1, RIGHT PAGE

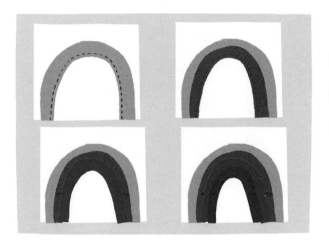 

3. Using the templates on p.138, cut out the rainbow pieces from different-coloured felt. Starting with the largest piece, pin and stitch in place, referring to the spread 1 diagram on p.21, leaving a 1cm/½in gap at the bottom of the page. Stitch the underside of the curve only, allowing the top of the curve to freely flap about.

Repeat with the other 3 rainbow pieces, in diminishing size order, slightly overlapping them as you go, so that only the stitching of the final (smallest) curve is visible.

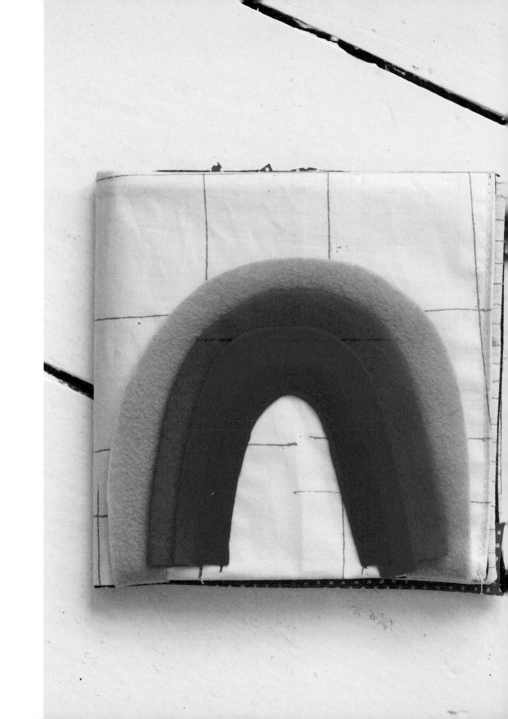

SPREAD 2, LEFT PAGE

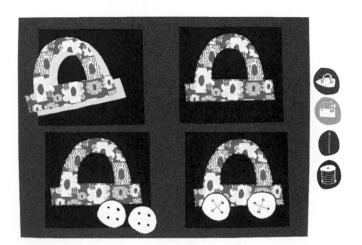

SPREAD 2, RIGHT PAGE

4. Prepare your selected 'car' fabric with adhesive webbing and, using the template on p.139, cut out the car. Position on the left-hand side of your spread 2 fabric, referring to the spread 2 diagram on p.21, and iron to fix. Topstitch all the way round to secure, stitching as close to the edge as possible.

Sew on the buttons for wheels.

5. Freehand embroider the tree trunk with brown thread, referring to the spread 2 diagram on p.21. I used a straight stitch and the regular foot on the sewing machine for this, as it's a simple 'up and back lots of times, slightly wonkily'-type affair. Stitch a horizontal line at the bottom of your trunk, as 'ground'.

Prepare your 'leaf' fabric by backing with iron-on interfacing. A light cotton, such as shirting fabric or cotton lawn, is ideal for this and the interfacing will prevent fraying. Cut out leaf shapes using the template on p.139.

Secure the leaves in place with a single line of stitching across each one, so they are free to flap. I found it easiest to lay a few at a time into position and feed them through the sewing machine randomly, adding more as I went, until the tree was in full leaf.

SPREAD 3, LEFT PAGE

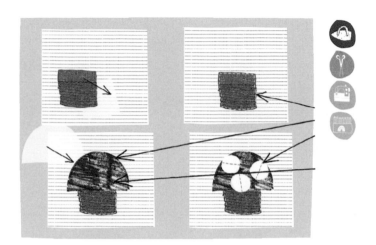

SPREAD 3, RIGHT PAGE

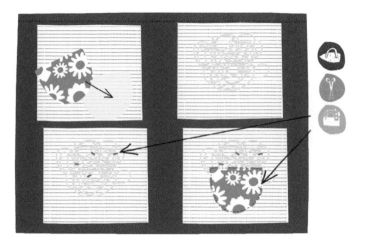

6. Prepare spread 3 by stitching turquoise-coloured horizontal lines across the full width of the ecru fabric, every ½cm/¼in, to create a 'lined paper' effect.

If you like, roughly pin-tuck some brown fabric (see p.11), creating a tactile 'gill' effect (or use flat brown fabric). Back the 'stalk' fabric, pin-tucked or not, with adhesive webbing and cut out a stalk shape using the template on p.139.

Prepare your 'toadstool cap' fabric with dye sticks (see p.12), then back it with adhesive webbing. Alternatively, use red fabric. Cut out a cap shape using the template on p.139.

Iron the stalk in place, referring to the spread 3 diagram on p.21, and topstitch all around to secure, as close to the edge as possible, then repeat with the cap.

Cut 6 spots from felt, using the template on p.139. Layer the spots in pairs on top of the toadstool and stitch in place down the middle, so they can flap freely.

7. On the right-hand side of your spread 3 fabric, make a nice swirly noodle nest with the string, referring to the spread 3 diagram on p.21, and secure in place by stitching in random places here and there, so that the loops of string are still free to twiddle with, but will not pull out completely.

Prepare your 'bowl' fabric with adhesive webbing and cut out, using the template on p.139. Position the bowl over the noodles, and iron to fix. Topstitch all around to secure, as close to the edge as possible.

SPREAD 4, LEFT PAGE

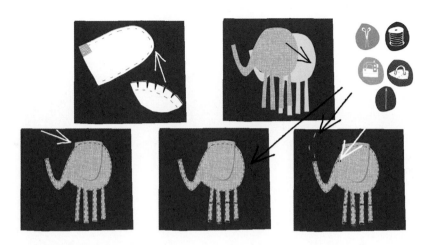

8. Cut out 2 elephant ear pieces using the template on p.140, place them right sides together and stitch around the curve, leaving the top open. Clip the curve. Turn out and press.

Back the 'body' fabric with adhesive webbing. Cut out the elephant body shape using the template on p.140 and iron into position, referring to the spread 4 diagram on p.21, and slotting the open end of the ear into place underneath the body as you do so.

Flopping the ear down, topstitch all the way around the body to secure (going over the ear where it meets the body), stitching as close to the edge as possible.

Freehand embroider the tail, knees and feet with brown thread. As for the tree trunk earlier, I used a straight stitch and the regular foot on the sewing machine. Freehand embroider some water splashes, squirting out of the trunk in turquoise. Finally, hand-embroider the eyes.

SPREAD 4, RIGHT PAGE

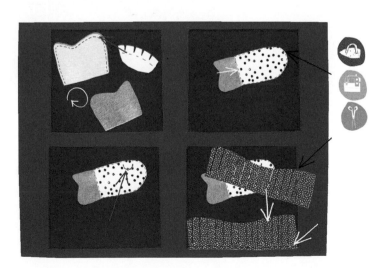

9. Prepare your 'fish body' and 'fish eye' fabric, backing it with adhesive webbing. Use the templates on p.140 to cut out the shapes.

Cut 2 tail pieces, using the template (I used a bit of gold lamé for the tail – snazzy fish!) on p.140. Place right sides together and stitch around 3 sides, leaving the end open as shown. Clip the curves, turn out and press.

Position and iron the body into place, referring to the spread 4 diagram on p.21, trapping the open side of the tail underneath as you do. Topstitch all around the body to secure, stitching as close to the edge as possible.

Position and press the little eye into place. Topstitch to secure.

Cut out the seaweed piece using the template on p.140, then snip vertical lines into the fabric, all the way along at regular intervals, leaving it intact by about 1cm/½in at the base, to create free-flowing greenery. Stitch the seaweed in place along the bottom of the page.

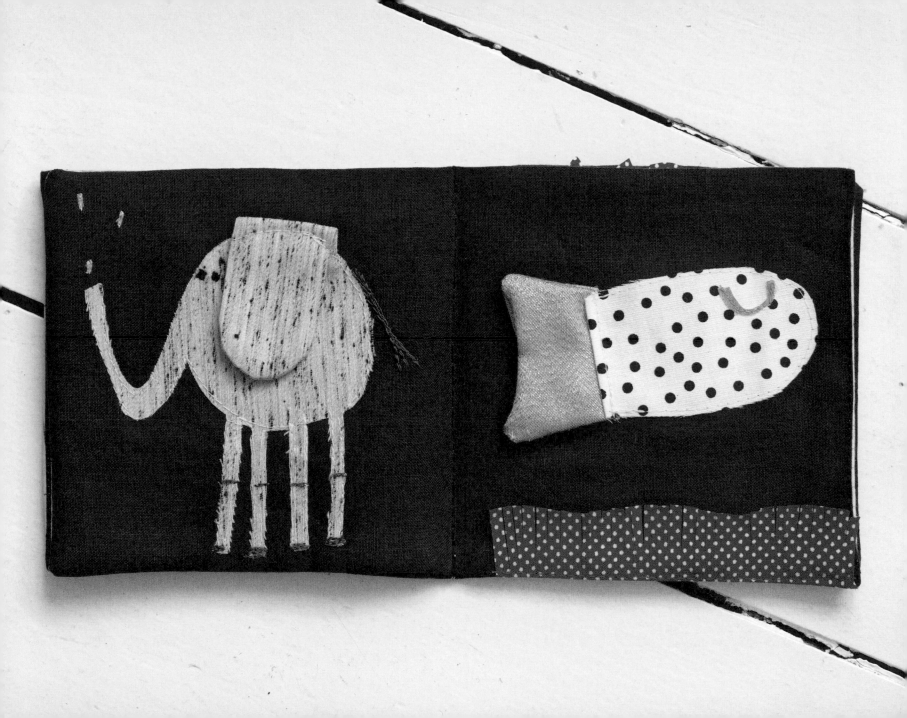

note

This is what the finished book will look like once you've sewn it all together.
Turn over for instructions.

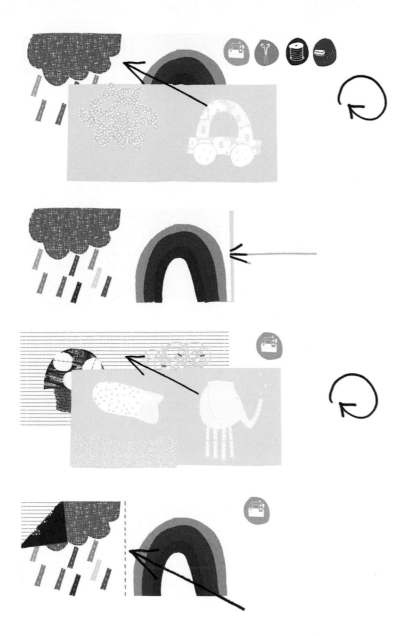

PUTTING IT ALL TOGETHER

10. Place spreads 1 and 2 together, right sides facing, and stitch on 3 sides, leaving one short side open. Turn out and press, taking time to roll the seams as you go so that it is fully turned out (see p.10).

Turn the open ends in by ½cm/¼in and press.

Cut your scrunchy plastic sheet to size, so that it slots inside the pocket. Slot into place, then sew up the open end, stitching as close to the edge as possible.

Repeat for spreads 3 and 4, omitting the plastic stuffing. Once turned out and pressed, topstitch along the bottom of the seaweed to hold it in place.

Lay spreads 1/2 on the table, tree/car-side up, then lay spreads 3/4 directly on top, fish/elephant-side up. Pin and stitch together down the centre line, vertically.

The end.

mobile

This is one of the very first things I made for my eldest mini. I have a thing about cardboard – I teach a LOT of mini workshops with it. There is something good and 'recyclably' pleasing about taking a redundant cardboard box, slathering it with paint and turning it into something fun. It also has a wonderfully 'doodled' feel when cut and painted.

from the toolbox

things you need

- Corrugated card (approx. 50 x 50cm/20 x 20in – can be in bits)
- Craft knife
- Cutting mat (or old magazine)
- White emulsion paint (a small jar)
- Selection of coloured paints (acrylic or emulsion)
- 2 x paint brushes (1 small, 1 medium)
- Colouring pens and pencils
- Embroidery thread (I used white)
- Large needle
- 2 strips of wood (approx. 25 x 1 x 1½cm/10 x ⅜ x ⅝in)
- Hot glue gun and glue sticks
- Strong string, for hanging

1. Using a craft knife and cutting mat, cut out the rainbow, sheep, bird, car, wheels, mushroom, mushroom spots, house, trees and leaves from the corrugated card, using the templates on p.132.

For the car and the house, cut out and discard the windows.

2. Paint all the shapes with a base coat of white emulsion. Cover the front side first, leave to dry, then repeat on the other side. Prepare your wood strips at the same time, covering with 2 coats of white emulsion. Set aside to dry.

Give the shapes a second coat of paint in colour, again working from front to back. Get creative, using up whatever you have available – bold colours are the key. The small brush, colouring pens and pencils are handy here for details such as the bird's beak, legs and the branches on the half-moon tree. Leave to dry.

3. Using the glue gun, stick the leaves onto both sides of the oval tree, the spots onto both sides of the mushroom, the wheels onto both sides of the car and the door onto the front of the house (slightly to the right of the door hole).

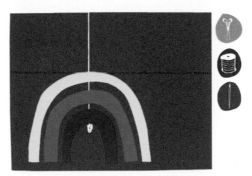

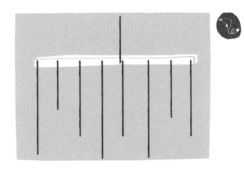

4. Using the needle and thread, join the rainbow pieces together by knotting the thread onto the smallest section, then threading the other 2 pieces on top, passing the needle and thread through the holes in the walls of the cardboard. Twist each section a little, so they are a bit 'higgledy-piggledy'. Leave a long piece of thread at the top for hanging later (30cm/12in ought to do it).

Thread up all of the other pieces, securing them well and leaving nice long threads for hanging.

5. Lay the threads on top of the first wood strip, making them different lengths and spacing them evenly across so that they will hang down freely. In the middle, position a long piece of strong string to come out of the top, this will be used to hang the mobile. Be generous with this piece, as it can always be trimmed to the desired length later on. Using spots of hot glue, secure the threads and string in place and leave to dry.

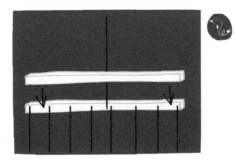

6. With your second wood strip at the ready, hot glue the length of the first wood strip (with the threads on) and sandwich the second wood strip firmly on top. Leave to dry.

And that's it! All you have to do now is decide how to suspend your mobile. It could be hung from a ceiling hook, or you could use a wooden arm specifically made for hanging mobiles from cots, which are available online.

embroidered cushion

This is a classic case of a bit of 'mixed media' taking a simple doodle to different heights – here, digital printing, stitching and appliqué create the finish on this cushion. My design of dancing minis can be digitally printed (see details for buying on p.143), or freehand embroidered (see template on p.133), if you prefer.

from the toolbox

things you need

- Main fabric – either digitally printed with my design (see p.143) or plain mid-weight cotton/linen (44 x 77cm/17½ x 30in)
- Black thread (if freehand embroidering image)
- Grey fabric dye stick (if freehand embroidering image)
- White and turquoise cotton thread
- Scraps of appliqué fabric for the clothing (optional)
- Iron-on adhesive webbing (optional)(50 x 50cm/20 x 20in)
- Cushion pad – I used a feather-filled pad (33 x 43cm/13 x 17in)

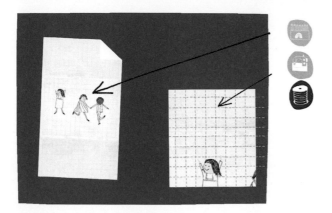

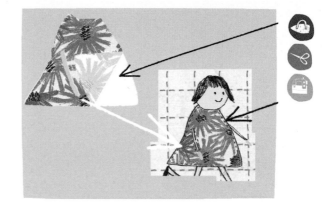

1. Prepare the design. If you are freehand embroidering the image, transfer the design on p.133 onto the centre of your main fabric (see p.11). Draw the scribble-shadow lines with the grey dye stick onto the centre of the cloth, using the photograph on p.35 as a guide. Iron to fix, then embroider the figures in black thread (see p.10).

Across the full length and width of the fabric, stitch turquoise lines to create the large 'graph-paper squares' pattern. If you are using my digitally-printed fabric, do this step to enhance the printed lines. Don't stitch over the printed figures.

2. Using the design on p.133 as a guide, make clothing for the little dancers. Attach adhesive webbing to the back of your patterned fabric of choice and cut to size. Iron into position and topstitch all around to secure, stitching as close to the edge as possible. You may also want to freehand embroider additional details, such as arms or buttons, in black thread over the top of the clothing, to finish.

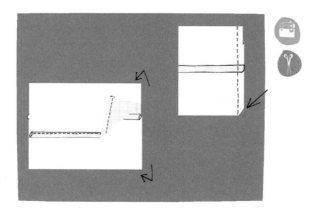

3. Hem the top and bottom (short) edges of the cushion fabric: turn the edges in twice to the wrong side by ½cm/¼in, then press and stitch.

Fold the fabric, right sides together, so that the embroidered design on the front of the cushion is central and the cushion is 33cm/13in tall. The back panels should overlap, creating an 'envelope' opening for the cushion. Stitch the two side edges together, each with a 1cm/½in seam. Trim the corners, turn out to the right side and press. Place cushion pad inside cover.

sleep sack

Whoever invented these was a genius – they are great once your mini one gets to around 6-months old and starts kicking off the sheets in the night. They are also easy to make, this one especially: just cutting, sewing and then the WONDROUSLY quick, super-duper 'poppering' with snap pliers. This sleep sack has been designed with an open base for ventilation. If you prefer it to be closed, just continue the poppers around the bottom.

You can use various fabrics for different levels of cosiness. For a cool sleep sack (for summer), use a light cotton (poplin or similar) of around 120gsm for the lining and outer fabrics. For a mid-weight sack, use the same lightweight lining with a cotton fleece fabric (330gsm) outer. For very cold weather, use cotton fleece (330gsm) for the lining and outer.

For a quirky design feature (and to quilt the outer and lining fabrics together), I've stitched a bright turquoise grid all over the front and back panels, and, using a remnant of patterned fabric, I've appliquéd my mini one's initial to the front panel.

I've included templates for small, medium and large sleep sacks, but the simplicity of the pattern means they can easily be adjusted by adding a few cms to the length or width, depending on the size of your mini one. Just keep the neckline the same as the original template (s, m or l).

from the toolbox

things you need

- Lining fabric – see project introduction for type (1 x 2m/1 x 2yd)
- Outer fabric – see project introduction for type (1 x 2m/1 x 2yd)
- Cotton thread (turquoise colour)
- Scrap of patterned fabric (optional)
- Iron-on adhesive webbing (optional)
- Snap pliers and 8 x plastic poppers/ snap fixings (or 12 if you are closing the base too)

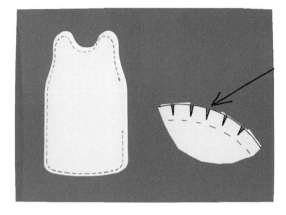

 1. Cut the lining and outer panels for the front and back, as indicated, using the templates on p.142.

For the front panels, with right sides of the outer and lining together and the front fabric on top, stitch a 1cm/½in seam all around, leaving a 10cm/4in gap on the right-hand side for turning out. Repeat for the back panels, but make sure that the back fabric is on the bottom when you stitch and, again, the gap for turning out is on the right-hand side. Clip the corners, turn out and press.

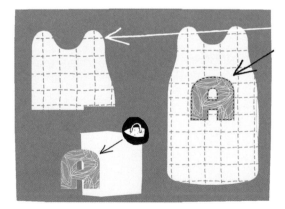

 2. Stitch a grid in turquoise thread all over the front panel (I stitched 4cm/1½in squares) for a quilted effect. I used a straight machine stitch for this. Repeat for the back panel.

If using, back your scrap of patterned fabric with the iron-on adhesive webbing and cut out your initial letter (if you need a template then a super-enlarged letter, in a font of your choice, printed out from the computer, works well). Place onto the front panel (making sure the open seam is on the right-hand side) and topstitch all around to secure.

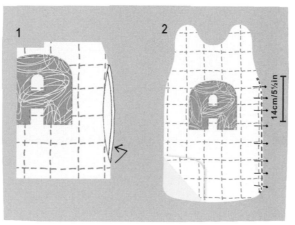

3. Lay your front piece on top of the back piece (outside out, making sure the open seams are on the right-hand side), lining up the base and sides. Turn under the raw edges on the two open seams.

Starting 14cm/5½in down from the top of the shoulder strap on the front piece, pin along the right-hand side until you get to the bottom right-hand corner (see diagram). Stitch a seam as close to the edges as possible, to join them together. Press.

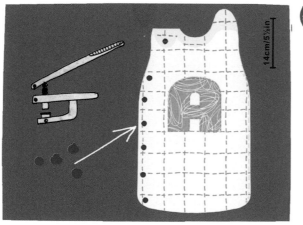

4. Mark-out where the poppers will go, lining up one on each shoulder strap. Then measure out 6 poppers at regular intervals between the start (14cm/5½in down from the top of the shoulder strap on the left-hand side of the front panel) to the bottom left-hand corner. (If you are closing the base, measure out an additional 4 poppers all the way to the right-hand corner.) Using your super snap pliers, fasten the poppers in place. Alternatively, you can of course hand-stitch these.

And that's it. One sleep sack sorted!

lollipop puppets

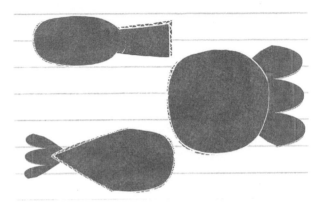

Let the mini ones put on a show! We made 3 fish puppets for an under-the-sea extravaganza, but these puppets are easily adaptable to other animals. The minis can decorate, but an adult will need to help with the cutting and glueing. The Pop-Up Shop (p.78) doubles-up as a puppet theatre.

1. Get your minis to draw 3 fish shapes, then you can cut out the shapes from corrugated card.

You will need

- Corrugated card
- Scissors
- 3 thin dowels, approx. 60cm/24in in length (or straight-ish sticks from the park)
- White emulsion paint
- Paint brushes
- Coloured paint
- Crayons
- Coloured paper
- Glue OR hot glue gun and glue sticks

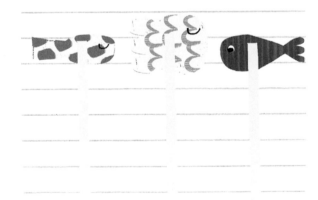

2. Paint the shapes white all over (you can also paint the dowels at this point) and leave to dry. Once dry, with coloured paint or crayons, or cover with a collage of cut-out, coloured-paper shapes. Using glue (or the glue gun), secure a dowel to the back of each puppet.

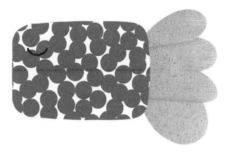

**perfectly
practical**

storage basket

This is a mini essential. I can say nothing more.

I've given measurements for small, medium and super-sized versions, to accommodate all your storage needs!

I've left this basket plain, but you could add appliqué letters or words to the side of the basket too, describing its contents. If you choose to do this, use up your scraps, or colour-in some fabric yourself, then back it with adhesive webbing (see p.11). Stitch to your main fabric panel before making up the basket.

from the toolbox

things you need

- Heavyweight cotton canvas fabric (see sizes below)
- Double-corrugated cardboard (see sizes below). This type of cardboard has two layers (two walls) of corrugated card, so is stronger and more rigid. If you can't find it, use two sheets of ordinary cardboard.
- A heavyweight fabric needle for your sewing machine
- Heavy-duty cotton thread
- Coloured paint, for the base
- Paint brush

Small

- 2 x fabric handle pieces (30 x 14cm/ 12 x 5½in)
- 1 x fabric panel piece (93 x 40cm/ 36½ x 15½in)
- 1 x fabric base piece (31-cm/12½-in diameter circle)
- Double-corrugated cardboard (29-cm/ 11½-in diameter circle)

Medium

- 2 x fabric handle pieces (30 x 14cm/ 12 x 5½in)
- 1 x fabric panel piece (125 x 50cm/ 49 x 20in)
- 1 x fabric base piece (41-cm/16¼-in diameter circle)
- Double-corrugated cardboard (39-cm/15¼-in diameter circle)

Super-sized

- 2 x fabric handle pieces (30 x 14cm/ 12 x 5½in)
- 1 x fabric panel piece (188 x 60cm/ 74 x 24in)
- 1 x fabric base piece (61-cm/24¼-in diameter circle)
- Double-corrugated cardboard (59-cm/23¼-in diameter circle)

top tip

You could also use heavyweight 3mm/⅛in thick felt, which won't need the edges turning and stitching. The handle pieces would be half the width stated, if so.

top tip

Make a homemade compass to draw large circles easily. Take a piece of thick string and push a nail or thumb tack through it to make the compass point. Measure your required circle radius (half the diameter) along the string and at that point push the tip of a sharp pencil or pen through the string. Holding the nail/tack firmly, you can now draw your circle onto your paper or fabric.

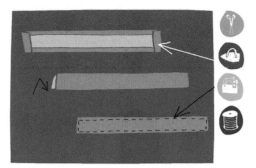

1. First make the handles. Take your first piece and turn the edges over by 1cm/½in all around. Press. Fold in half lengthways and stitch all around, as close to the edge as possible. Repeat for second handle.

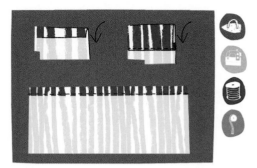

2. Next make the sides of the basket. Fold one long edge of the main panel over by 1cm/½in, then again by 3cm/1¼in. Press and stitch to secure. This will be the top edge of the basket.

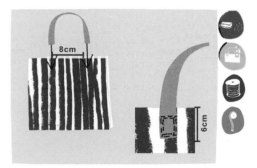

3. Fold over a 1cm/½in seam down each short edge of the panel piece. Press to mark the seam allowance. Fold the panel in half, wrong sides together, with both seam allowances tucked inside.

Position the ends of your first handle centrally on the top edge of the folded panel, 6cm/2½in down from the edge, and with a gap of 8cm/3in between each end. Make sure the handle is not twisted. Pin in place, turn over and repeat with the second handle. Stitch the end of each handle to the panel in a square shape (twice round for strength), to secure.

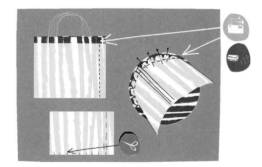

4. With the right sides together, join the sides of the main panel with a 1cm/½in seam. Clip notches along the bottom raw edge, slightly less than 1cm/½in deep. Right sides together again, pin the base panel in place (a bit fiddly, but you will get there) and stitch a 1cm/½in seam to join. Clip the base piece all round the circle and turn out.

Paint your cardboard base in a colour of your choice, allow to dry, then slot into the base of the basket, pushing all the fabric tabs underneath. Fill with toys.

fish pencil case

A super cool fishy pencil case, for all of those colouring pencils!

from the toolbox

things you need

- Medium-weight cotton or linen fabric (50 x 50cm/20 x 20in)
- Scrap of fabric for the tail (I used some vintage gold lamé)
- Zip (20cm/8in)
- Zipper foot for sewing machine
- Cotton thread (dark brown for eye)

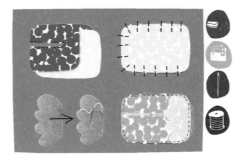

1. Using the templates on p.136, cut out 2 x body pieces and 2 x tail pieces. Cut one of the body pieces into 2 pieces lengthways, at roughly ⅓ of the width.

With the tail pieces right sides together, stitch a ½cm/¼in seam as shown, leaving the straight side open. Cut notches on the curves. Turn out and press.

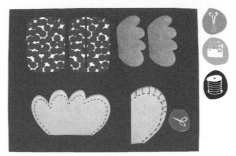

2. On the straight sides of the back body pieces, turn a ½cm/¼in seam to the wrong side and press. Using the zipper foot on your sewing machine, attach the zip (see p.12).

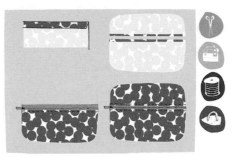

3. With the zip half open (for turning out later), place the front and back body pieces right sides together. Pin all around, leaving the tail end open.

Make 2 small pleats in the tail and slot into the open end of the case, making sure all the raw edges are together. Pin in place.

Stitch all around, allowing a 1cm/½in seam, securing the tail as you go. Turn out and press.

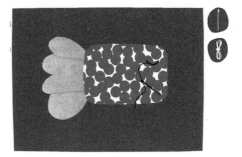

4. Embroider an eye (as shown) with dark brown cotton thread. I used a back stitch, moving back and forth 5–6 times to make a heavy line.

Voila!

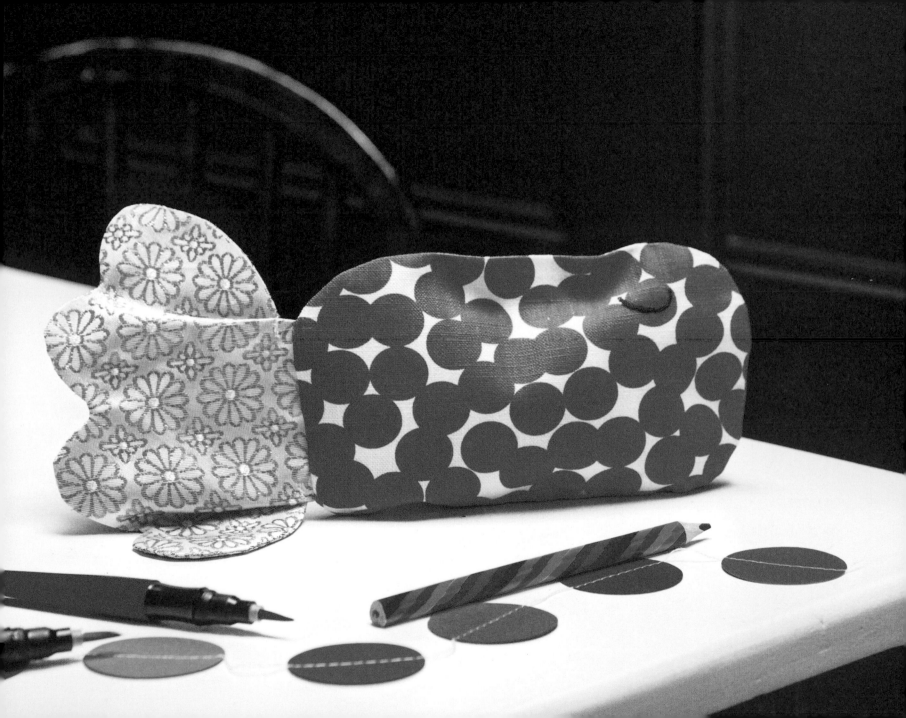

baby-changing pouch

Being well-versed in the art of carrying nappies and diapers around, I have found a double pouch to be a lifesaver. It is PERFECT for housing a few nappies and wipes on one side and the very essential emergency change of clothes in the other. The secret central slip pocket is handy too, for tissues, disposal bags or anything really… When well stocked, it's super easy to seize and shove into any decent-sized baby bag, backpack or handbag. A 'grab and go' if you like. It also works as a very nice non-baby-bits bag too.

from the toolbox

things you need

- Outer fabric – medium/heavyweight cotton/linen (50 x 100cm/20in x 1yd)
- Lightweight cotton lining – 126gsm poplin or similar (50 x 100cm/20in x 1yd)
- 2 x open-ended zips (30cm/12in)
- Zipper foot for sewing machine
- Cotton thread
- 3 x small binder clips

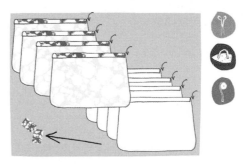

1. Using the template on p.141, cut 4 x pattern pieces from outer fabric. Cut 2 x small pieces for zip-ends, 1½cm x 3cm/½ x 1¼in.

Cut 4 pattern pieces from lining fabric.

On the lining and outer fabric pieces, fold in 1cm/½in at the top to the wrong side and press.

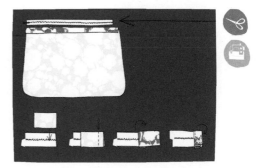

2. Trim the zips to size, making them 1cm/½in shorter than the length of the top of the bag. Stitch the zip-end pieces to the ends of the zips (see p.12).

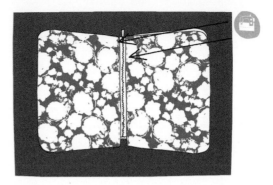

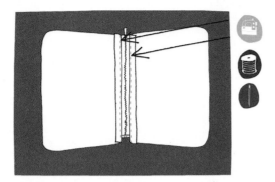

3. Using the zipper foot on your sewing machine, take 2 lining pieces and prepare to attach them to a zip, one each side. The zip should be right side up. The lining should be wrong-side up. Line up the turned edge of the lining with the edge of the zip, positioning the lining edge ½cm/¼in away from the teeth. Pin and topstitch through all the layers of fabric/zip. Repeat on the other side.

4. Place 2 outer fabric pieces onto the zip right-side up, placing the turned edge of outer fabric as close to the zip teeth as possible to hide the lining fabric. Topstitch each side to the zip as in Step 3.

Repeat Steps 3 and 4 for the other zip and lining/outer pieces.

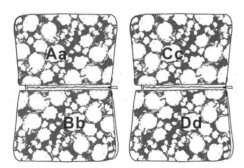

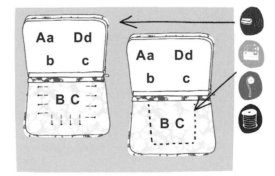

5. This is a fiddly bit, but take it slow, pin well and you will be fine! You need to make one pouch first, turn it out, then make the second one. I have labelled the pieces Aa, Bb, Cc and Dd to help (uppercase for the outer fabric, lowercase for the lining). Here goes… Place the two pieces in front of you to match the diagram, making sure the closed zips are facing in the same direction.

6. Place outer B on top of outer C, right sides together, making sure the zips are facing the same direction. Line up and pin B to C (keep Aa/Dd and b/c out of the way as you are pinning). In pencil, on the wrong side of the fabric, lightly mark a pocket, H12 x W15cm/H4¾ x W6in, centred and starting 1cm/½in down from the zip. Stitch the 3 sides of the pocket through both layers of fabric, back-stitching at the start and finish, for strength. Remove the pins.

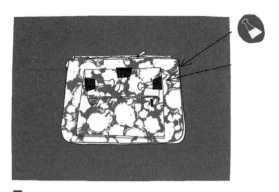

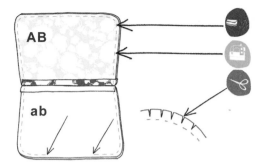

7. Laying the, now attached, pouches back on the table, fold all the sides down below the zips. Gather up and fold in the edges of Cc and Dd and clip neatly together with binder clips, folding the arms down to secure. This keeps them out of the way while you are sewing up the first pouch.

Make sure the zips are lined up correctly with each other. This is really important. If there are any wonky bits, you want them at the base of the pouch, not on the zip. The base is easy to neaten up.

It's also important to half open the zips at this stage, otherwise you will be stuck when you come to turn out the pouch.

8. Place outers A and B right sides together (trying to ignore the folded Cc/Dd pouch – it will tuck inside for now) and lining a and lining b together (the zip should be in the middle). Pin each pouch all around, leaving a 10cm/4in gap at the base of the lining pieces.

Starting at the base of the lining, stitch the seams together as shown (remembering to leave the gap). It gets quite fiddly when you get to the zip – I find turning the sewing machine wheel by hand helps here. Stitch as near to the zip end as you can and be careful to stitch the open end of the zip into the seam when you get to the other side. Snip a few notches into the round corners.

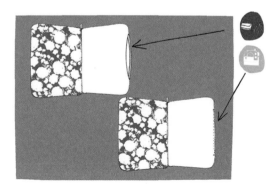

9. Turn out (the Cc/Dd pouch will emerge at this point). Fold in the edges of the gap at the base of the lining and sew up the seam. Stuff the lining into the bag and push the seams into the corners.

Repeat Steps 8 and 9 for pouch Cc/Dd, folding and clipping pouch A/B neatly away and trying your best to ignore it.

Hooray! You should now have a turned-out and stitched-up double pouch, complete with central pocket! Press, fill with nappies/diapers and you are away!

lunch bag
(and other bits & bobs)

This is a great little bag and, if my minis are anything to go by, it will be a VERY well-used great little bag too. It's pretty straightforward to make, if you take a little bit of time over the corners. They always look more complicated than they are. Do a few test runs on some scrap fabric if you need practice first.

from the toolbox

things you need

- Medium-weight cotton or linen fabric (50cm x 1m/20in x 1yd is plenty)
- Cotton thread
- Piece of plastic (e.g. from an ice-cream tub lid) or rectangle of cardboard (9 x 19cm/3½ x 7½in) (optional)

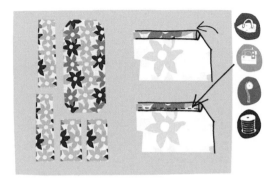

1. Using the templates on p.141, cut 1 x main piece, 2 x side pieces and 2 x handles from your fabric. On the main piece, fold the short edges over twice to the wrong side, each time by ½cm/¼in. Press and stitch.

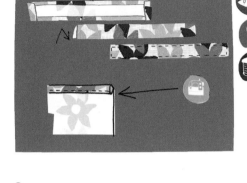

2. Take your first handle piece and turn the edges over by ½cm/¼in all around. Press. Fold in half lengthways, press and stitch all around, as close to the edge as possible. Repeat for second handle.

On each side piece, fold 1 short side over twice to the wrong side, each time by ½cm/¼in. Press and stitch.

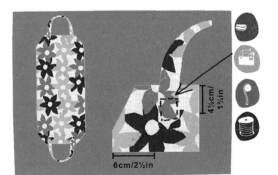

4½cm/1¾in

6cm/2½in

3. Pin and stitch the handles to the right side of the main piece (see diagram for positioning) in a square shape (twice round for strength), to secure.

4. With the right sides together, pin and stitch the side pieces to the main piece, as shown, taking care on the corners. I find it easiest to stop at the corner, needle down, lift the presser foot and swivel, adjusting the fabric slightly to line up again, then continue on the new straight line.

Trim off the corners, turn out and press.

Add a fabric-covered plastic or cardboard base if you like. Slot the base into the bag and it is complete!

treasure map

A fun project for a rainy or sunny day. An outdoor treasure map is the norm, but I've made an indoors map, for those experiencing a downpour or who don't have outside space.

1 Choose a room for your treasure hunt.

2 Make a 'treasure chest', filling an old box or tin with goodies. Hide it.

3 On a 40cm/16in square piece of paper, or whatever you have to hand (brown parcel paper is perfect for this), draw in key bits of furniture and obstacles. Add a trail to follow and an 'X' marks the spot.

4 Fold up the map a number of times, each time really rubbing the crease flat to make it look as though it's been folded up for ages. Unfold it and, for an aged look, rough it up a bit with a very light rubbing of sandpaper, pumice stone, damp teabag or candle wax.

5 Set the mini ones off on a treasure hunt!

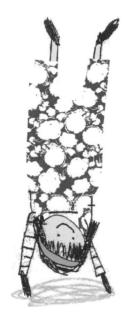 washing line

apron

What can I say? This is an essential piece of kit. It is most useful when worn for baking, making, painting, gardening, watering, building, 'playdoh-ing'…

It's also REALLY easy to make and (to quell the upset I went through when I was little and aprons were TOO BIG and got in the way of scooping the leftover cake mix out of the bowl) this one has ties for the neck, rather than a far-too-big loop.

from the toolbox

things you need

- Mid-weight cotton/linen (50 x 80cm/ 20 x 31½in)
- Cotton webbing for ties (2m/2yd will be more than enough)
- Cotton thread

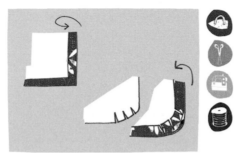

1. Cut out the apron and pocket piece, using the templates on p.131. For the apron piece, turn the edges ½cm/¼in to the wrong side all the way round. Press, turn over another ½cm/¼in, and press again.

For the pocket piece, clip the curve and turn the edges ½cm/¼in to the wrong side all the way round. Press. Turn over the top straight-edge again by ½cm/¼in. Press. Stitch the top seam.

2. Cut the webbing into 2 x 50cm/20in lengths and 2 x 40cm/16in lengths. Turn one end of each piece in by ½cm/¼in twice, press and stitch.

Tuck the raw ends of the ties into the seam of the apron, positioning them as shown in the photograph opposite. The 50cm/20in ties are for the waist; the 40cm/16in ties are for the neck. Pin, then stitch the apron all around, securing the ties in place as you go. Press. Then, fold back the ties and topstitch flat so they lie outwards rather than inwards.

3. Pin the pocket into position, as shown in the photograph, and stitch round 3 sides, as close to the edge as possible, leaving the top open. Stitch 2 small diagonal lines at each top corner of the pocket, for strength.

gym bag

A handy little bag for swimming stuff, sleepover bits and general mini-bag fodder perfect for age 4 and up! It neatly loops over the shoulders like a backpack, for comfortable carrying, too. Easy to make, roomy and useful.

from the toolbox

things you need

- Cotton half panama or drill fabric (80 x 28cm/31½ x 11in)
- 6mm/¼in cotton cord, 2 pieces (70cm/27½in each)
- Cotton thread
- 2 x regular safety pins and 1 x large safety pin (nappy/diaper pin)
- Bodkin

1. Lay your fabric in front of you and turn the top and bottom edges (short sides) over to the wrong side by ½cm/¼in and press. Cut 4 clips in the raw side edges, each one 2cm/¾in deep, 6cm/2⅜in down from the hem on all 4 corners.

Above the clips, turn the fabric edges in to the wrong side by 1cm/½in, then 1cm/½in again. Press and stitch.

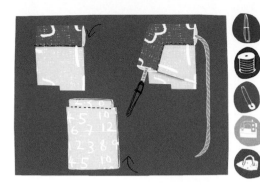

2. Fold the top and bottom edges in to the wrong side by 3cm/1¼in. Press and topstitch, to create the cord casing. Fold the main panel in half, right sides together. Secure at the top with safety pins. Attach the large safety pin to the end of the first cord and thread the other end through the bodkin. Thread the cord through the channel (both sides) and loosely tie the ends. Repeat for the second cord, threading it through from the opposite side.

3. Pin the side seams on both sides, starting 3cm/1¼in from the bottom, until you reach the start of the cord casing. Stitch a 1cm/½in seam. Turn out, then turn in the edges of the gaps at the base by 1cm/½in and press.

4. Take the ends of the cords and sandwich them in-between the two layers of fabric in the bottom corners of the bag. Pin in place. Topstitch over the corners, closing the holes and securing the cords in place as you do so – I went back and forth a few times for strength. Press and get packing!

'brousers' (baggy trousers)

We love a 'brouser' (or baggy trouser) in our house – and these ones should fit ages 12–18 months. They are great for all seasons (depending on the fabric) and large enough to accommodate a bulky nappy/diaper, too. I used a light cotton poplin here, ideal for summer. Use a cotton drill, fine wool or soft denim for colder days. The French seam allows for a neat turn-up, until your mini one's legs grow.

from the toolbox

things you need

- Fabric (50cm x 1m/20in x 1yd)
- 3mm/⅛in baby elastic (30–40cm/12–16in)
- Cotton thread
- Large safety pin (nappy/diaper pin)
- Bodkin

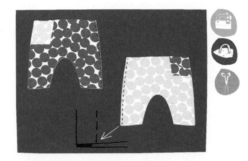

1. Using the template on p.129, cut 2 x pattern pieces and put one piece on top of the other, wrong sides together. Pin, then stitch down one side, allowing a ½cm/¼in seam. Trim seam a little.

Turn the pieces right sides together, press the seam, and stitch along the same side again, creating a ½cm/¼in French seam, enclosing your first seam. Press.

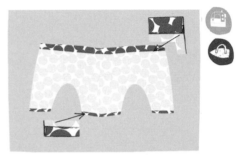

2. Turn down the top edge twice, by ½cm/¼in then 1cm/½in, and press. Stitch, as close to the edge as possible, to make a channel for the elastic.

Hem the trouser bottoms, turning a ½cm/¼in seam to the wrong side twice. Press and stitch.

3. Fold back along the first side seam, with wrong sides together, and stitch around the gusset arch, allowing a ½cm/¼in seam. Trim seam a little, turn out to right sides together and press. Stitch around the gusset again, creating a ½cm/¼in French seam. Press.

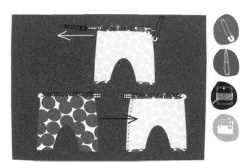

4. Measure your mini one's waist and cut the elastic to the same size. I used 30cm/12in. Secure a large safety pin to one end of the elastic and thread the other end through a bodkin. Thread the elastic through the channel (the safety pin will stop it disappearing into the channel). Test out on your little one and adjust accordingly. Pin or tack the ends of the elastic in place.

With wrong sides together, pin and stitch the second leg seam, allowing a ½cm/¼in seam, securing the elastic as you go by stitching back and forth a few times. Trim excess fabric on the seam, turn to right sides together and press. Stitch along the same side again, creating a ½cm/¼in French seam. Turn out, press again and that's it!

romper

I LOVE a romper. They are SUPER cute, and roomy and elasticated too, which means they last just a little bit longer on fast-growing mini folk. I have lined this one to make it cosy for chillier days (worn with tights), but it is great unlined too for warmer days (without tights!). I made the one in the photograph with 126gsm cotton poplin (outer and lining fabric), but have also successfully used a 255gsm cotton drill (with a lighter-weight cotton lining) for this pattern.

This pattern is 12–18 months. For 9–12 months, reduce width and height measurements by 2cm/¾in; for 18–36 months, add 2cm/¾in to the width and 4cm/1½in onto the length.

from the toolbox

things you need

- Outer fabric – printed/coloured cotton (50cm x 1m/½ x 1yd)
- Lightweight cotton lining – 126gsm poplin or similar (50cm x 1cm/½ x 1yd)
- 3mm/⅛in baby elastic (1m/1yd is plenty)
- Cotton thread
- 2 x small buttons
- Snap pliers and 3 x plastic poppers/snap fixings
- Safety pin
- Bodkin

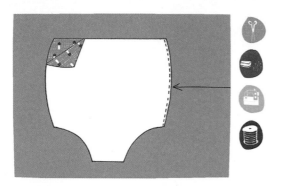

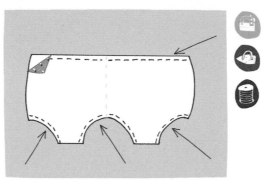

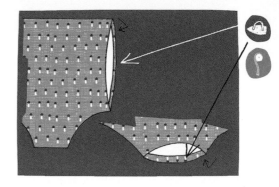

1. Lay out the outer fabric and fold in half, right sides together. Using the template on p.141, cut 2 x body pieces in one go and 2 x straps.

In the same way, fold the lining fabric right sides together and cut 2 x body pieces in one go.

Place the 2 outer body pieces right sides together, and stitch down one side, ½cm/¼in from the edge. Repeat for the lining pieces. Press the seams open (which is tricky, as they are curved, but bear with it!).

2. Lay the outer piece on top of the lining piece, right sides together, and stitch a ½cm/¼in seam across the top and around the curved leg edges, as shown. Turn out and press, taking time to roll the seam as you go, so that it is fully turned out (see p.10).

3. Turn in the open sides ½cm/¼in and press. Turn in gusset pieces 1cm/½in and press.

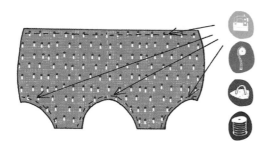

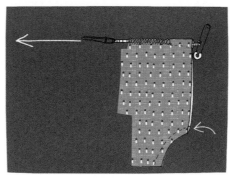

5. Measure your mini one's chest and cut the elastic to the same size. I used 30cm/12in. Thread it through top channel. I use a safety pin at the end of the elastic to stop it threading all the way through, and a bodkin to guide the front end through the channel. Secure in place at both ends, stitching back and forth over the elastic 2 or 3 times.

Measure your mini one's thighs and repeat for the 3 leg channels. I used 21cm/8in of elastic for the middle channel and 10½cm/4in for each of the side channels. Secure in place at both ends, stitching back and forth over the elastic 2 or 3 times.

4. Turn over 1cm/½in to the wrong side along the top edge and the curved leg edges. Press. Stitch close to the turned edge to create a channel for the elastic.

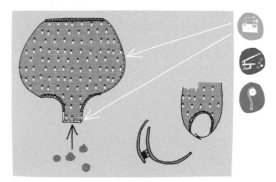

6. With right sides facing, stitch the remaining side edges together, allowing a 1cm/½in seam. Stitch both gusset seams, stitching as close to the turned edges as possible. Secure 3 poppers/snaps to each gusset, so that the front gusset overlaps the back gusset. I used my favourite new toy, the snap pliers, to fix them – they are amazing (see p.12).

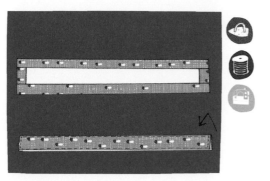

7. Turn the edges of each strap piece over by ½cm/¼in all around. Press. Fold in half lengthways, press and stitch all around, as close to the edge as possible.

8. Hold your fabric taut and pin and sew the straps to the inside back of romper, about 8cm/3in in from the side seam (but measure your mini one to get the placement exact).

9. Make buttonholes at the front of the romper to line up with the straps (see Basics chapter, p.11, for technique). Stitch buttons onto the straps in the desired position after measuring on your mini (these can be adjusted as your mini one grows).

overalls

I really like these, so much so that I might have to make a pattern for a grown up. They are great for kids. They can frolic about and focus on the important task in hand… being little.

This pattern is for an average-sized 3-year-old but can be sized up or down. To adapt the pattern, for each year of age difference add or subtract 2cm/¾in onto/from the width and 4cm/1½in onto/from the length (see templates on p.134). For a scaled-down version (when your mini is still in nappies/diapers), I would turn the hem on the inside leg and add poppers/snap fixings to close instead of stitching.

You can change the weight of the cloth to make these suitable for summer or winter. Made in a twill or fleece, they work well over the top of a layer or two for the colder months. In a lightweight cotton, they are perfect for warmer climes with a loose t-shirt beneath.

things you need

- Cotton twill, fleece or mid-weight cotton/linen (for cooler months); cotton poplin, plain or lightweight linen (for warmer days) (1 x 1.2m/1 x 1.2yd)
- Cotton thread
- Snap pliers and 2 x plastic poppers/snap fixings

from the toolbox

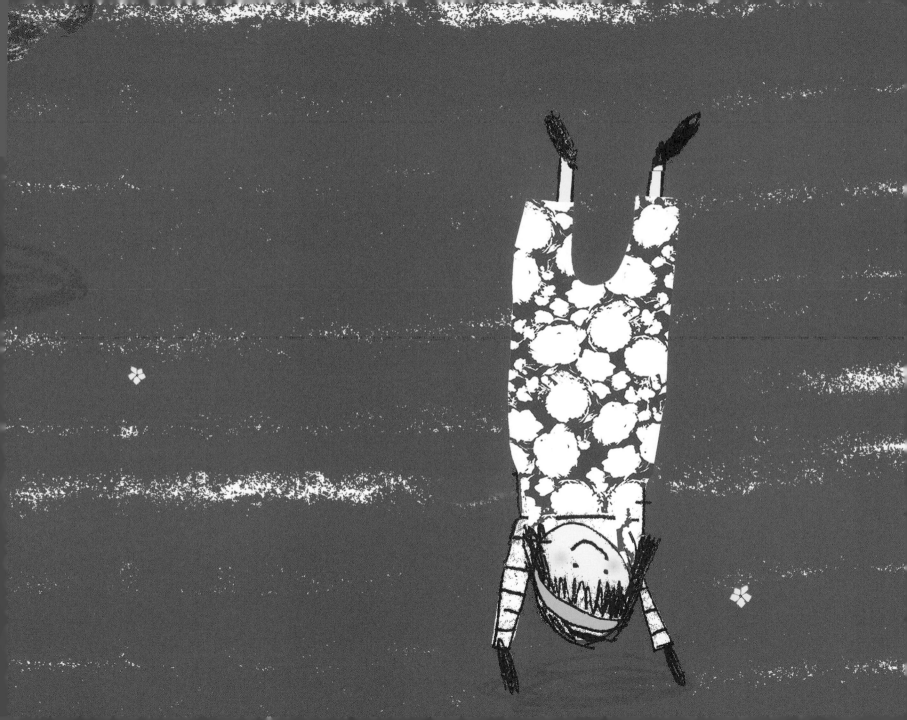

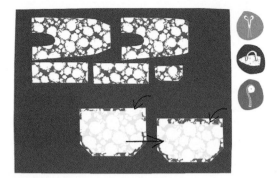

1. Cut 1 x front panel, 1 x back panel, 1 x pocket and 2 x straps, using the templates on p.134.

On the pocket, turn the edge in by 1cm/½in to the wrong side all around and press. Turn again by 1cm/½in, along the top (straight edge) only this time. Press.

2. On the front panel, make two 2cm/¾in clips on either side edge, 10cm/4in down from the top. Above the clips, starting on the right-hand side, turn the side edge in by 1cm/½in to the wrong side, then turn down the top edge by the same amount, then turn in the left-hand side edge. Press. Repeat for a second time. Press again. Turn the bottom edges in by 1cm/½in to the wrong side, then turn 1cm/½in again. Press.

3. On the back panel, turn the top edge down by 1cm/½in, then again by 1cm/½in. Press. Repeat for the bottom edges.

On the straps, turn the edges in by 1cm/½in to the wrong side all around and press. Fold in half lengthways and line up the edges. Press.

Stitch the seam on the top of the pocket, the top of the back panel, the bottom hems, and all round on the straps (as close to the edge as possible on the straps).

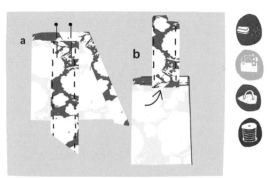

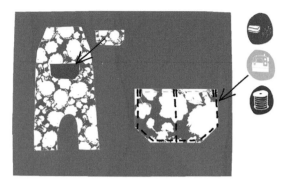

4. On the front panel, with the wrong side facing you, slot the straps into either side of the seam at the top and pin in place. Stitch the turned seams at the top of the front panel, securing the straps in place as you do so. Flip the straps up, press and pin, then topstitch all along the top edge to secure them again.

5. Pin the pocket in place and stitch round 3 sides, as close to the edge as possible, leaving the top open. Then stitch from top to bottom of the pocket down the centre, creating a double pocket. Add extra stitches at the 3 places where the top of the pocket meets the main fabric, for strength.

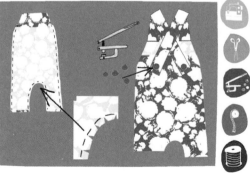

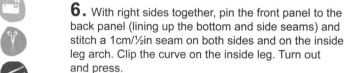
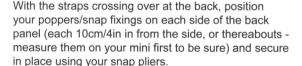

6. With right sides together, pin the front panel to the back panel (lining up the bottom and side seams) and stitch a 1cm/½in seam on both sides and on the inside leg arch. Clip the curve on the inside leg. Turn out and press.

With the straps crossing over at the back, position your poppers/snap fixings on each side of the back panel (each 10cm/4in in from the side, or thereabouts - measure them on your mini first to be sure) and secure in place using your snap pliers.

And there you have it. Overall, I'm sure you've done a great job! (Dad joke… sorry.)

chalkboard photobooth

This is a super cute way to take fun snaps of your little ones. All you need is a bit of chalk and a decent-sized chalkboard (1m²/1yd² is ideal). If you don't have a chalkboard, simply paint some cardboard/hardboard/mdf/chipboard with chalkboard paint.

Chalk up some doodles on your board and lay it down on the floor. Then lay your mini one in position and snap away!

Here are some ideas…

bobble hat

snapping crocodile

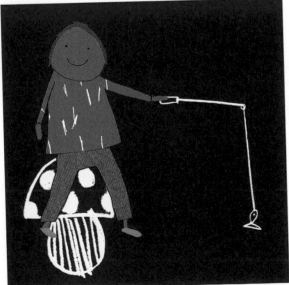

toadstool and fishing rod

74

butterfly

crown

lion

play time

pop-up shop

We LOVE 'playing shops'. There are some wonderful 'all-singing, all-dancing' toy shops on the market, but they're often quite pricey. This one requires only card, paint and a little bit of time. Once made, it can be hung from a door frame whenever the urge to make a shop comes along. It flattens down, so doesn't take up half of your living room when not in action (we slot ours away behind a cupboard). And it doubles as a great theatre for puppet shows (see p.40). The kids will LOVE it! You'll need to make the shop, but the minis can help you cook up things to sell.

things you need

- Any door frame in your home (to house the shop front)
- 2 x enormous cardboard boxes
- Craft knife
- Chalkboard paint (250ml/8fl oz)
- White emulsion paint
- Paint brushes
- 2 x 5cm/2in screws
- Screw driver
- 4m/4yd rope (8 or 10mm/^{5}/$_{16}$ x ^{3}/$_8$in diameter)
- 2 x small tables, stools or upturned boxes
- Chalk

1. Measure the width of your door frame and the height of your minis, then cut a piece of cardboard to that width x a height that will suit (taller than the minis, with enough room for a window). Cut out a window in the middle for your little ones to 'man the shop' from (make sure they can see out!). Paint the front with chalkboard paint and set aside to dry.

2. Cut a second piece of cardboard, half the height of the shop front and the same width – this will be the shop awning. Paint black and white vertical stripes, 10cm/4in wide, all along the awning and set aside to dry.

3. Once the awning is dry, cut out a scalloped shape at the bottom of each stripe along one edge.

4. Lay the awning on top of the shop front piece with both painted sides facing up. In each of the top corners of the front and the awning make a hole and thread a 60cm/24in (or shorter/ longer, depending on height of door frame) piece of rope through each hole from back to front, making a large knot to secure.

5. For the awning piece, make two holes in the bottom corners and thread two 1m/1yd lengths (or a bit longer if needed) of rope through each hole, this time knotting on the rear side.

6. Line up the ropes with the top of the door frame and screw a couple of screws into the top of the door frame where the ropes will meet It – these will need to stick up by at least 3cm/1¼in. Hook the shop front and awning top ropes in place, tying them so that the bottom of the shop front hangs just above the floor. Hook the bottom awning ropes up so that it hangs at a 45°angle to the shop front (or thereabouts).

Chalk up whatever you are selling on the front of your shop, pop a stool or table in front, and one behind for the cash register. Display your goods and open up shop!

things to sell

The little ones can help to make these, depending on how mini they are! We made 'chocolate dipping' sweet treats for our shop. Messy, but fun!

To make 'biscuit faces' (we used homemade cookies but bought ones would work too), dip the end of each biscuit into melted chocolate for hair, then pipe a smiley face onto each one. To make 'biscuit butterflies', dip pairs of mini pretzels into melted chocolate, then attach your 'wings' to a chocolate finger biscuit. Obviously, it was a chocolate shop that day, but the groceries on pp.80–87 are great for the pop-up shop too.

dip

pipe

dip

stick

groceries

These little grocery bits are SUPER easy to make and great fun for your mini ones to line the shelves of their pop-up shops with. You don't need a snazzy 'shop front' to play shops – just a little table, a pretend till, some stock and paper carrier bags will do the trick. If you fancy making a little bit more effort and have a spare cardboard box lying about, then the Mini Make on p.78 shows you how to make a pop-up 'doorway' shop, complete with awning!

from the toolbox

things you need

- Felt squares in a variety of blues (2 or 3), greens (3), grey (1) and cream (1) (20 x 20cm/8 x 8in)
- Plain white cotton fabric (1 x 1m/1 x 1yd)
- Cotton thread
- Fabric dye sticks (pink, brown, orange)
- Stuffing (I used leftover bits of cotton fabric, which I rolled into a sausage and cut into thin ribbons)
- Fish tail – shiny blue fabric (20 x 20cm/8 x 8in)

turnip

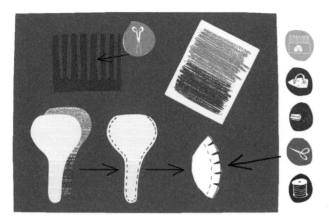

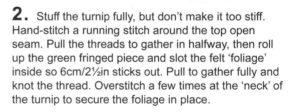

1. Cut a piece of green felt, 10 x 8cm/4 x 3in. Along one of the long sides, cut 6cm/2½in vertical slits, ½cm/¼in apart. This can be fairly imprecise, as this gives a more 'natural foliage' effect.

Cut a 30 x 20cm/12 x 8in piece of cotton fabric and 'colour-in' the bottom half with a brown dye stick, and the top half with pink. Iron to fix.

Fold the coloured-in fabric in half lengthwise, with right sides together. Using the template on p.130, cut 2 x 'turnip' pieces in one go. Pin and stitch a ½cm/¼in seam all around, leaving the top seam open. Clip the curves and turn out. Press the seams. Turn the open top seam into the wrong side by ½cm/¼in and press.

2. Stuff the turnip fully, but don't make it too stiff. Hand-stitch a running stitch around the top open seam. Pull the threads to gather in halfway, then roll up the green fringed piece and slot the felt 'foliage' inside so 6cm/2½in sticks out. Pull to gather fully and knot the thread. Overstitch a few times at the 'neck' of the turnip to secure the foliage in place.

One turnip done! To make more, try using the template as a guide and 'free-styling' a bit to add variety to the turnip shapes and colours.

carrot

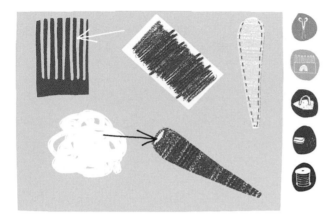

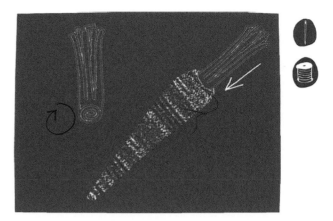

1. Cut a piece of green felt, 10 x 12cm/4 x 4¾in. Along one of the short sides, cut 10cm/4in vertical slits, ½cm/¼in apart. This can be fairly imprecise, as this gives a more 'natural foliage' effect.

Cut a 20 x 20cm/8 x 8in piece of cotton fabric and 'colour-in' with an orange dye stick. Iron to fix.

Fold the coloured-in fabric in half lengthwise, with right sides together. Using the template on p.130, cut 2 x 'carrot' pieces in one go. Pin and stitch a ½cm/¼in seam all around, leaving the top seam open. Clip the curves and turn out. Press the seams. Turn the open top seam into the wrong side by ½cm/¼in and press.

2. Stuff the carrot fully, but don't make it too stiff. Hand-stitch a running stitch around the top open seam. Pull the threads to gather in halfway, then roll up the green fringed piece and slot the felt 'foliage' inside so 10cm/4in sticks out. Pull to gather fully and knot the thread. Overstitch a few times at the 'neck' of the carrot to secure the foliage in place.

One carrot complete!

celery

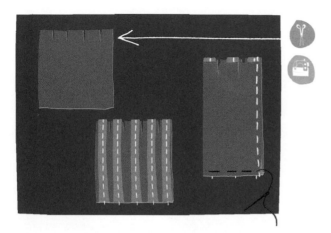

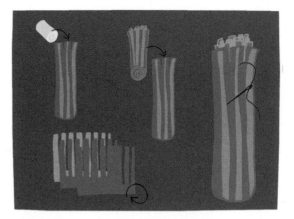

1. Cut a piece of green felt, 14 x 14cm/ 5½ x 5½in. Cut 7 or 8 pieces of another shade of green, 1 x 14cm/½ x 5½in (ish). Place these at regular intervals onto the square piece of felt and stitch each strip vertically down the middle to secure. In between each stitched strip, snip a 3cm/1¼in slit.

With right sides together, fold the green square in half so the strips are vertical and stitch a ½cm/¼in seam down one side to join the edges. Hand-stitch a running stitch around the bottom open seam. Pull to gather the base and stitch to secure. Turn out.

2. Take a 5 x 10cm/2 x 4in (or thereabouts) piece of felt (any shade of green will do), roll into a sausage and stuff into the base of the celery.

Take 3 pieces of felt (approx. 8 x 7cm/3¼ x 2¾in) – I used 2 green shades and a cream. Along the long sides, cut 10cm/4in vertical slits, 1cm/½in apart (ish). Lay the pieces on top of one another and roll into a sausage. Stuff this into the hollow of the celery, to sit on top of the base stuffing, and stitch to secure. And that's it!

mushroom

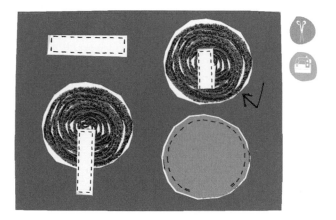

1. Cut a rough 11cm/4½in circle (the more imprecise the better) out of the plain cotton fabric. Use this as a template to cut the same shape out of grey felt.

Using a circular line (as if drawing the rings of a tree trunk) draw the mushroom gills onto the cotton fabric, with alternate black, brown and grey fabric dye sticks. Layer the colours up until the base is fully covered. Iron to fix.

2. Cut a 4 x 8cm/1½ x 3¼in piece of cream felt. Fold in half along the long side and stitch all around, close to the edge, to create a flat stalk. Position on the 'gill' side of the cotton circle and stitch into place. Fold up the stalk inside and, with right sides together, pin and stitch the gill and felt circles together, leaving a gap of 5cm/2in for turning out.

Turn out. Loosely stuff, then turn in the edges of the opening and stitch to close. One mushroom made!

fish

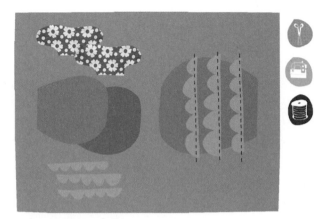

1. Fold the 'tail' fabric in half, right sides together, and using the template on p.130, cut 2 tail pieces in one go from the shiny blue fabric. Cut 2 x body pieces from different tones of blue felt using the template on p.130.

Using another blue felt colour (if wished), cut 4 strips (14cm/5½in long and about 4cm/1½in wide – each one can be a slightly different width), cutting a scalloped wave into one long side on each. One at a time, starting two-thirds of the way across, lay a scalloped strip onto one of the main body pieces and stitch down the straight side to secure, allowing the scalloped edge to flap freely. Repeat with the next strip slightly layering the scalloped edge over the first piece. Continue with the other 2 strips.

2. With the two tail pieces right sides together, stitch the tail all around, allowing a ½cm/¼in seam and leaving the straight side open. Turn out and press.

With the two body pieces right sides together, stitch the body all around, allowing a ½cm/¼in seam and leaving the straight side open. Turn out and press. Turn in the open seam by ½cm/¼in and press.

Using black thread, hand-embroider an eye onto the fish (my fish was sleeping!).

Stuff loosely. Slot the open end of the tail into the open end of the fish body. Pin and stitch to close, securing the tail in place as you go. Then the fish is finished!

dressing-up *hats*

A dressing-up box is KEY for me, as part of the playroom fodder. It's GREAT fun! I made the sheep version of this, for my eldest daughter at Halloween, a few years ago. I haven't seen a little one yet who doesn't look SUPER CUTE in an outfit like this. It's still a regular go-to from the dressing-up box, which is a compliment of the highest order!

To make a body to go with it, I used the Romper pattern on p.67 (without the elastic around the top and legs) in the same faux-sheepskin fabric. You can switch the fabrics and ear shape on this basic bonnet to make different animals. The patterns are for a sheep, bear and chicken, but let your imagination run wild!

from the toolbox

sheep and bear hats

things you need

- Outer fabric – faux-sheepskin for the sheep; brown towelling or an old white towel, dyed chocolate brown for the bear (50cm x 1m/ 20in x 1yd)
- Lining – cotton fabric: grey for the sheep; black or brown for the bear (50cm x 1m/20in x 1yd)
- Cotton thread

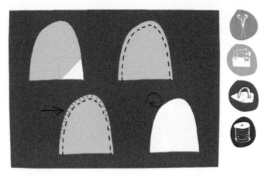

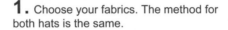

1. Choose your fabrics. The method for both hats is the same.

Folding your outer fabric right sides together and using the templates on p.130, cut 2 x bonnet pieces and 2 x ear pieces in one go, then cut 1 x standard central panel. Repeat for the lining fabric.

With right sides together, pin and stitch the first ear pieces (one lining, one outer) with a ½cm/¼in seam, leaving the flat end open. Clip the curves, turn out and press. Repeat for the second ear.

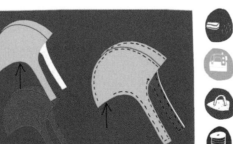

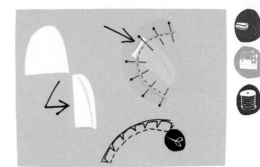

2. With right sides together, pin the first outer bonnet piece to the outer central panel as shown. Fold the first ear in half vertically and slot it into the seam, 6cm/2½in from the front of the bonnet. Stitch, allowing a 1cm/½in seam, then clip the curve. Repeat on the other side with the second bonnet piece, sewing the second ear into the seam as you go. Press.

Repeat for the lining pieces, minus the ears.

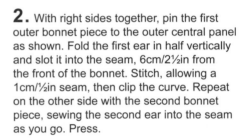

3. With right sides together, pin the lining to the outer by slotting it inside. Leave a gap at the base of the bonnet (10cm/4in) for turning out, and stitch all around, allowing a 1cm/½in seam.

Clip the curves. Turn out and press. Turn the opening in by 1cm/½in, press and stitch, stitching as close to the edge as possible.

chicken hat

things you need

- Outer fabric – white cotton, linen or towelling (50cm x 1m/20in x 1yd)
- Lining – white cotton fabric (50cm x 1m/20in x 1yd)
- Comb – red felt (30 x 30cm/12 x 12in)
- Cotton thread

1. Folding your outer fabric right sides together and using the templates on p.130, cut 2 x bonnet pieces in one go. Then cut 1 x chicken outer central panel piece, using the template on p.130.

Folding your lining fabric right sides together and using the templates on p.130, cut 2 x bonnet pieces in one go. Then cut 1 x standard central panel piece.

Cut the chicken's comb from the felt, using the template on p.130.

Cut the outer central panel piece in half lengthways as shown in the diagram. Place the 2 outer central panel pieces right sides together and sandwich the comb into place, with the long edges all lined up. Stitch together, allowing a ½cm/¼in seam. Press.

Now you have made the central panel with comb in the outer fabric, you can follow the rest of the instructions as for the Sheep/Bear Hat (Steps 2–3, minus the ears).

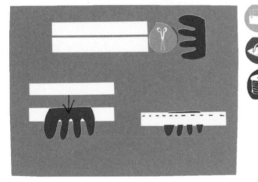

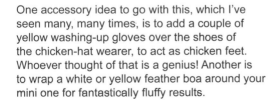

One accessory idea to go with this, which I've seen many, many times, is to add a couple of yellow washing-up gloves over the shoes of the chicken-hat wearer, to act as chicken feet. Whoever thought of that is a genius! Another is to wrap a white or yellow feather boa around your mini one for fantastically fluffy results.

crowns

These are really easy to make and a great addition to the dressing-up box. The colours and fabrics given here are just suggestions; simply by tweaking these elements, you can create lots of fun variations.

I have added a veil for one crown and a cape for the other. The crowns are designed to sit on the top of the head (like a party hat), so no need to worry about head measurements or anything like that.

from the toolbox

things you need

...with veil

- Cream 3mm/⅛in felt (30 x 8cm/12 x 3in)
- Ivory organza fabric (40 x 80cm/16 x 31½in)
- Ivory/ecru cotton fabric (16 x 8cm/6½ x 3in)
- Snap pliers and 8 x ivory poppers/snap fixings
- Gold elastic cord (30cm/12in)
- Gold lamé fabric (20 x 20cm/8 x 8in)
- Iron-on adhesive webbing
- Cotton thread

...with cape

- Brown 3mm/⅛in felt (30 x 8cm/12 x 3in)
- Turquoise or blue 1mm/¹⁄₃₂in felt (50 x 60cm/20 x 24in)
- Turquoise or brown cotton fabric (2 pieces, each 9 x 5½cm/3½ x 2¼in)
- Snap pliers and 4 x brown or black poppers/snap fixings
- Gold lamé off-cut (20 x 20cm/8 x 8in)
- Iron-on adhesive webbing
- Black or brown elastic cord (30cm/12in)
- Cotton thread

...with veil

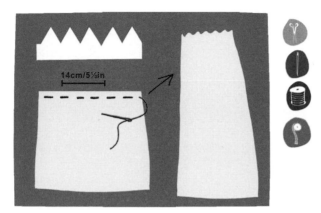 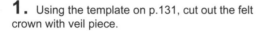

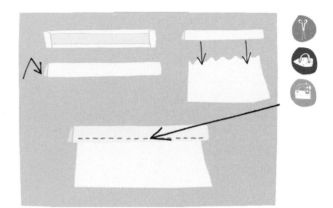

1. Using the template on p.131, cut out the felt crown with veil piece.

Take the piece of organza and, on one of the short ends, sew a loose running stitch all the way along. Pull the threads to gather it up, until it is 14cm/5½in wide. Set aside.

2. Take the small piece of cotton fabric and turn the edges in to the wrong side all around by 1cm/½in. Press, then fold in half lengthways and press again. Sandwich the gathered piece of organza in-between the folded fabric and stitch along the open edge to secure.

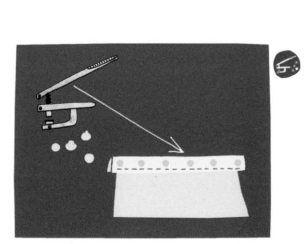 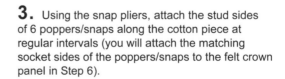

3. Using the snap pliers, attach the stud sides of 6 poppers/snaps along the cotton piece at regular intervals (you will attach the matching socket sides of the poppers/snaps to the felt crown panel in Step 6).

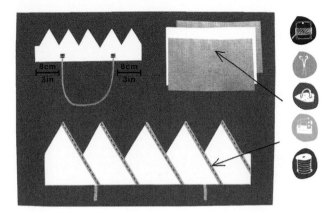

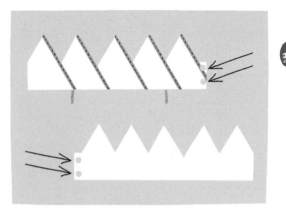

4. On the inside, 8cm/3in in from each side of the crown piece, secure each end of the elastic cord, stitching back and forth a few times.

Fix the gold lamé to both sides of the adhesive webbing so you have double-sided 'bonded gold' (this will prevent fraying when you cut it). Cut out 5 strips, about ½ x 11cm/¼ x 4½in. On the outside of the crown, stitch the gold strips onto the felt along the diagonal, as shown, stitching a line down the centre of each strip. Trim off the ends of strips if necessary.

5. Using the snap pliers, attach one side of 2 poppers/snaps to the 'popper tag' on the felt crown, then line up with the other side of the crown and attach the matching poppers/snaps.

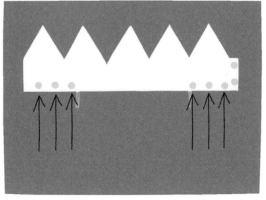

6. Lay the felt crown in front of you, right-side down. Lay the cotton piece of the veil down on top and mark where the remaining socket sides of the poppers/snaps need to go – 3 on either side along the bottom edge. Avoid marking poppers in the middle, which will become the front of the crown. Attach the socket sides of the poppers/snaps to the felt so the veil will snap into place on the inside of the crown.

Snap the crown together, then snap the veil to the inside. Now you are princess ready!

...with cape

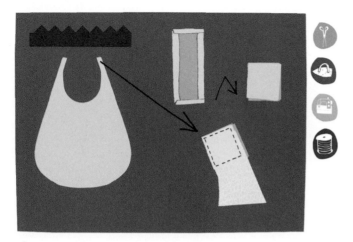

1. Using the template on p.131, cut out the crown with cape piece from the brown felt and cut out the cape piece from the turquoise felt.

Take the 2 small pieces of cotton fabric and turn the edges in to the wrong side all around by 1cm/½in. Press, then fold in half widthways and press again. Sandwich each end of the cape neck straps in-between one of the pieces of folded fabric and stitch all around each one to secure.

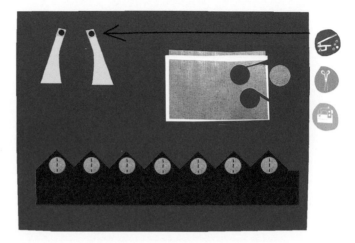

2. Using the snap pliers, attach one side of a popper/snap fixing to each of the covered ends of the cape straps, so that the straps can be joined.

Fix the gold lamé to both sides of the adhesive webbing so you have double-sided 'bonded gold'. Cut out 7 gold dots, about 2cm/1in in diameter. On the outside of the crown, stitch the gold dots onto each point of the crown, stitching a line down the centre of each – they should flap a little bit.

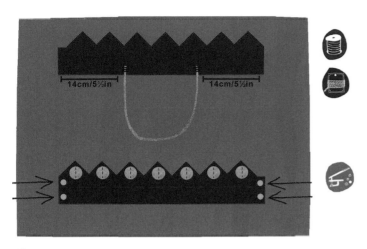

3. On the inside, 14cm/5½in in from each side of the crown, secure each end of the elastic cord, stitching back and forth a few times.

Using the snap pliers, attach one side of 2 poppers/snaps to the 'popper tag' on the felt crown, then line up with the other side of the crown and attach the matching poppers/snaps.

One crown and cape ready to dress up a princely prince!

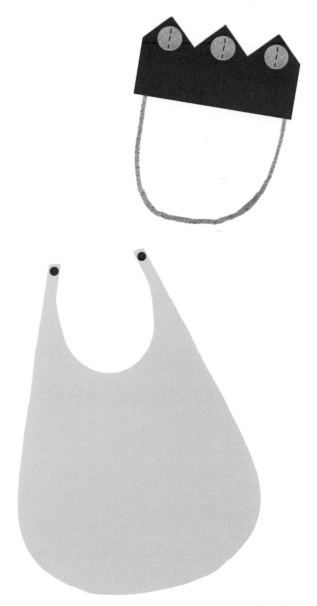

cardboard camera

This is super quick and seriously satisfying to make. It's also a great way put a second-hand box and postal tube to good use.

from the toolbox

things you need

- Double-corrugated card (5 main pieces cut to 12½ x 10cm/5 x 4in, plus 1 piece cut to 8 x 2cm/3 x ¾in, for the shutter button)
- Cardboard poster/postal tube (cut to 5cm/2in long), for the lens
- Fabric for strap (28 x 4cm/11 x 1½in)
- 12cm/4¾in length of paper-bag handle (the twisted-paper-string kind – found on posh gift bags), for viewfinder
- Hot glue gun and glue sticks
- White emulsion paint
- Black acrylic paint, or colours of your choice
- Paint brushes (1 x small for dots, 1 x medium for white paint)

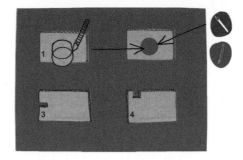

1. Number your 5 main card pieces. On piece 1: draw round the cardboard tube to mark out, then cut a hole for the 'lens' to slot into. Leave piece 2 as it is.

On piece 3: in the centre of one of the short sides, cut out a rectangle, 3cm/1¼in deep x 1½cm/½ in wide – this will form a groove for the strap.

On piece 4: on the top, long side, about 3cm/1¼in from the edge, cut out a rectangle, 3cm/1¼in deep x 2cm/¾in wide – this will form a groove for the shutter button to sit in.

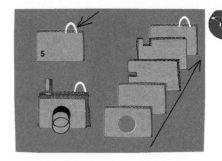

2. Bend your 'viewfinder' piece of paper string into a loop shape, apply hot glue to the ends, then slot into position on the corrugated edge of main piece 5 (see diagram for position).

Starting with main piece number 5 at the bottom, align and glue the main cardboard pieces together, using a generous application of hot glue for each layer.

Apply hot glue to the end of the poster/postal tube 'lens' and slot into place in piece 1. Slot the shutter button piece into the groove in piece 4. Leave to set.

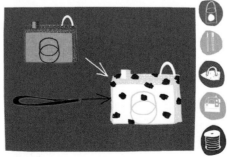

3. Paint the camera white all over and leave to dry. Decorate with colours and patterns of your choice (or with black spotty splodges as I have). Leave to dry.

Following Step 7 on p.69, press and stitch a fabric strap. You can leave the ends raw-edged as these will be hidden within the camera.

Finally, hot glue the strap in place and leave to set. Now you're ready to encourage a fledgling photographer to get snapping!

cardboard car

A play car… who doesn't have fun in one of these? This one has a little retro horn too, what's not to love?!

This car is designed for your little one to sit inside, or to 'drive' around by holding it up by the handles and zooming about with it (in a wide-open space far away from obstacles, obviously!). It fits a little one aged about 3, but you can adjust to suit the size of your mini, with a bigger or smaller box.

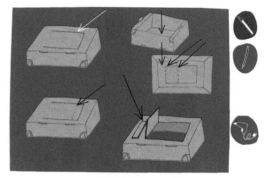

things you need

- Large, sturdy, cardboard vegetable box (mine was L80 x W40 x H30cm/ 31½ x 16 x 12in)
- Pencil
- Ruler
- Craft knife
- Double-corrugated cardboard (2 x large boxes/sheets)
- Hot glue gun and glue sticks
- Sheet of fine sandpaper
- Paint brush
- Paint (white emulsion and colours of your choice)
- Chalkboard paint
- Chalk pen
- 1 x retro air horn (available online)

from the toolbox

1. With the large vegetable box upside down, mark out in pencil a 60 x 30cm/24 x 12in rectangle in the centre of the base of the box. Then, 10cm/4in from one of the short ends, make a score line across the width of the rectangle with the craft knife (making sure not to cut right through the board). Cut out 3 sides of the rectangle to make a flap (the attached end should be furthest away from the score line).

Turn the box right-side up and make 2 more score lines with the craft knife (making sure not to cut right through the board): one along the attached side of the flap and one at 25cm/10in from the attached side. Both should be the full width of the flap.

Turn the box back over so it's upside down again. Fold the flap up along the attached fold line. Fold the flap behind and down towards the base at the 25cm/10in scored line, then fold out at the final score line, so the end of the flap sits flat on the base of the box. Hot glue this flap to the base (this will be the dashboard).

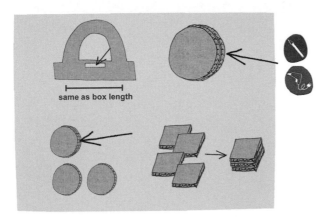

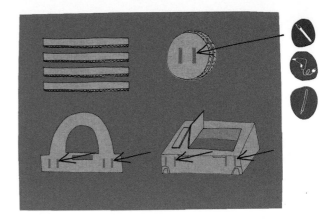

2. Using the car template on p.139 as a guide, draw a car shape onto a piece of cardboard, ensuring the bottom edge of your car is the same length as the length of your vegetable box. Cut out the shape. Draw a window, using the template for guidance, and then draw a handle (about 12 x 5cm/5 x 2in) just under the window. Cut out the window and handle. Draw round your completed car side on another piece of cardboard and cut out. You should now have two identical car sides.

Cut out 8 cardboard wheels, 40cm/16in in diameter (or 10cm/4in greater than the height of your box). Make the first wheel, layering up 2 wheel pieces. Hot glue together. Repeat for the other 3 wheels.

Cut out 4 x 20cm/8in cardboard circles. Hot glue 2 circles together, to make the steering wheel (the other 2 circles will be the headlights). Cut 3 pieces of cardboard, 4 x 4cm/1½ x 1½in, and hot glue together. Hot glue this block to the back of the steering wheel.

3. Cut 4 cardboard strips, 4 x 20cm/1½ x 8in. These will be gigantic 'stitches', used to join the car together… bear with me. On each wheel make two vertical slits, 4 x ½cm/1½ x ¼in, and 4cm/1½ in apart. Position the wheels onto the first car side panel and mark through the slits with a pencil. Cut the same slits into the car side. Repeat on the other car side.

Hold the first car side panel up to the side of the box, with the car side base lined up with the base of the box. Mark the slits through the car side onto the box and cut the same slits into the side of the box. Repeat on the other side of the box with the second car side panel.

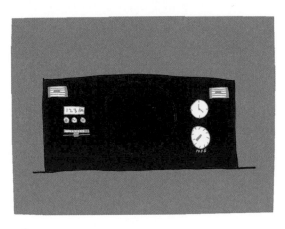

4. Before painting, lightly rub over all the edges with the sandpaper, just in case of sharp bits.

Paint all of the pieces, including the box, with the colours of your choice. Leave to dry.

Paint the dashboard with blackboard paint. Leave to dry. Add heater, clock, radio and speedometer details with the chalk pen.

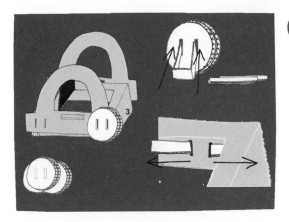

5. Assemble the car, starting by hot glueing the side panels in place, making sure the slits are lined up. Hot glue the wheels into position lining the slits up once again.

Take the cardboard strips and, one at a time, 'stitch' through the slits, hot glueing to the front of the wheel and pulling through tight to the inside of the box. On the inside of the box fold the strips out to the sides and hot glue in place.

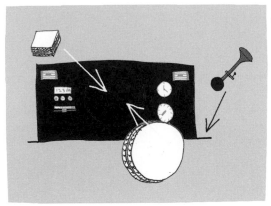

6. Hot glue the steering wheel to the dashboard, and the headlights to the front of the car.

Attach the retro horn to the right-hand side of the dashboard, or to the side of the car (depending on the type of horn you have, the attachment fixings tend to come included).

And that's it. Play car done! Brum brum!

hobby horse

I didn't have one of these when I was little, but since making this one, my daughter and I have been 'horse racing' round the house like complete loons.

from the toolbox

things you need

- A large cardboard box (or two), double-corrugated, if poss
- Fabric for the ears (I used some gold lamé scraps)
- Craft knife and cutting mat
- Sticky tape
- Paint – white, dark grey, brown and a bright colour for the dowel
- Paint brushes, various sizes
- Kitchen paper towels
- Hot glue gun and LOTS of glue sticks
- Grey yarn for the mane
- Wooden dowels – 2½cm/1in diameter (1m/1yd length and 25cm/10in length)
- Rope for reins (1m/1yd)

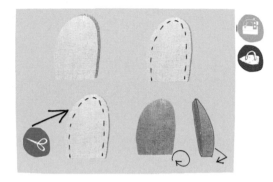

1. Using the template on p.137, cut 10 x horse head pieces out of cardboard and number each one, 1–10.

Cut 4 x ear pieces out of fabric, using the template on p.136. Place 2 ear pieces right sides together and stitch all around, allowing a ½cm/¼in seam and leaving the base open. Clip the curves, turn out and press. Repeat for the second ear.

2. Starting with head piece 1, draw round the handle dowel to mark out a hole for it to slot through, as shown. Cut out the hole using a 'star' technique, cutting from the edge of the marked circle into the centre, a number of times. Fold the cut pieces round to the wrong side and secure with tape, making a neat round hole.

For head numbers 2–9, cut a rougher circle as these won't be seen. To make sure the holes line up, go through one by one. Line up head piece 1 with head piece 2, then firmly press the dowel through hole 1 to make a mark on head piece 2. Roughly cut out the hole marked. Repeat this until every head piece has a handle hole.

Flip head piece 10 over, and use the 'star' cutting technique for a neater hole, as this will be seen.

Line up all the head pieces in order and do a 'dry run' with your dowel, to check the holes line up and adjust if necessary.

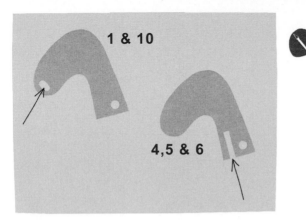

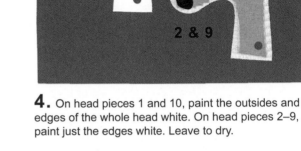

3. On head pieces 1 and 10, cut nostril holes freehand, as shown.

On head pieces 4, 5 and 6, cut a channel for the main dowel piece to slot into, as shown. Draw around the top of the dowel on head piece 4, cut out the shape marked, then use head piece 4 as a template to mark out and cut the same shape on head pieces 5 and 6.

4. On head pieces 1 and 10, paint the outsides and edges of the whole head white. On head pieces 2–9, paint just the edges white. Leave to dry.

On head pieces 2 and 9, paint an area of dark brown (which will show through the nostrils on pieces 1 and 10). Leave to dry.

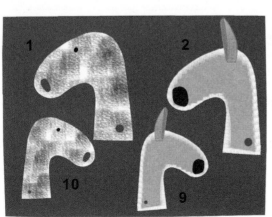

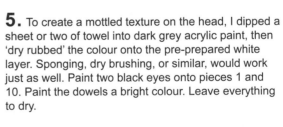

5. To create a mottled texture on the head, I dipped a sheet or two of towel into dark grey acrylic paint, then 'dry rubbed' the colour onto the pre-prepared white layer. Sponging, dry brushing, or similar, would work just as well. Paint two black eyes onto pieces 1 and 10. Paint the dowels a bright colour. Leave everything to dry.

On head pieces 2 and 9, hot glue the ears in place, folding each ear in half longways and sticking the open edge onto the cardboard head piece as shown.

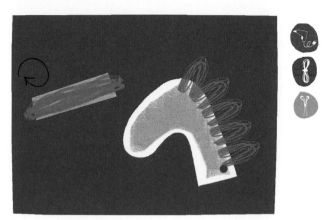

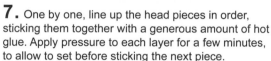

6. For the mane, I used loops of wool and attached them with the hot glue gun to head pieces 3–8. Wind the wool around a 30cm/12in (ish) piece of scrap cardboard 8 times, then remove and, holding the threads together, attach in 'U' shapes onto the head piece 3, starting just behind the ear position. Repeat until you reach the base of the neck. Then repeat on the remaining 5 head pieces (4–8), leaving the glue to set on each as you go.

Now you're ready to assemble everything.

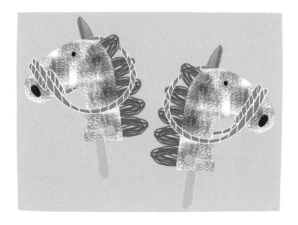

7. One by one, line up the head pieces in order, sticking them together with a generous amount of hot glue. Apply pressure to each layer for a few minutes, to allow to set before sticking the next piece.

Saw the painted handle dowel in half and insert into the channel. You want the 2 handle dowel pieces to meet in the middle of the head. Mark a small dot on the first handle half to indicate when it has been inserted half way. Remove and squeeze a generous dollop of hot glue into one side of the hole. Slot the marked handle halfway into the hole up to your guide mark. Hold to set, then repeat on the other side.

Squeeze a generous amount of hot glue into the channel for the main dowel and insert the pre-painted pole, holding in place for a few minutes, to allow to set.

8. Hot glue the rope for the reins in place (looping it around the nose – see diagram). Leave to set fully. Cut and trim loops of the horse's mane to your desired shape.

And that's it! Off you go... clip clop!

Pop-up forest

This is a fun way to bring drawings to life. I've taught lots of workshops using this technique and kids love it. You'll be on cutting and glueing duty and the mini ones can colour in the trees.

Things you need

- Double-corrugated card
- Craft knife and cutting mat
- Hot glue gun and glue sticks
- Scissors
- Coloured paint
- Paint brushes
- Scraps of paper (in shades of green and yellow)
- Oil pastels or paint sticks
- Wooden coffee stirrers

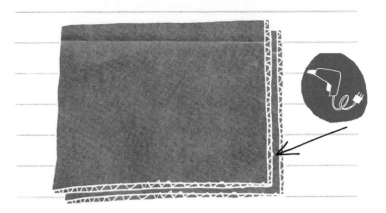

1. Cut three 40 x 40cm/16 x 16in pieces of cardboard. Using your hot glue gun, glue around the edges and sandwich the pieces together to make a forest floor.

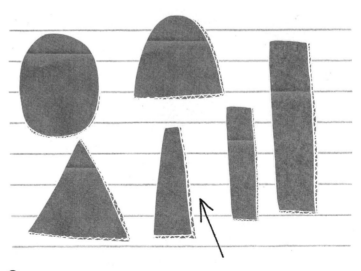

2. Cut out various tree-top shapes (6–8) and a variety of tree-trunk shapes (6–8) from the cardboard. Make sure the open holes of the corrugated card are at the base of the tree trunks.

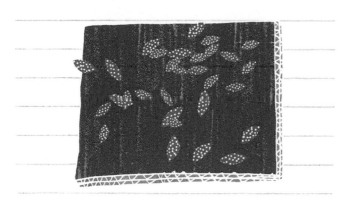

3. Paint your forest floor and leave to dry.

Meanwhile, cut out lots of little leaves from the paper. Once the forest floor is dry, scatter the leaves all over it and glue in place.

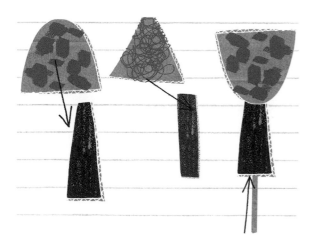

4. Colour-in your tree trunks and tree tops with the oil pastels. Glue the tree tops to the tree trunks and insert a coffee stirrer into the holes at the base of each trunk.

5. Choose places to 'plant' your trees and make small incisions in the forest floor with scissors or a craft knife. Slot the coffee stirrers of each tree into the incisions to secure.

super-sized fun

lion cushion

I once made a mini lion outfit for dressing-up in a similar vein to this – it was so easy and super effective that I thought it would be REALLY nice scaled up into a HUGE lion cushion. Here's how to do it.

I used a 250gsm cotton/linen for the main body of the cushion, but a cotton drill or heavyweight half panama fabric would work just as well. The lion's face has been digitally printed onto the fabric in the photo (see details for buying on p.143), but it could also be embroidered and coloured-in with dye sticks for a similar effect (see template on p.135).

things you need

- Front fabric – 250gsm cotton/linen, digitally printed with lion face OR off-white medium/heavyweight cotton/linen, to colour with dye sticks and embroider (60 x 60cm/24 x 24in)
- Fabric dye sticks (optional)
- Back fabric – medium/heavyweight cotton/linen (60 x 120cm/23½ x 47¼in)
- Brown felt (1m x 2½m/1 x 2¾yd is plenty)
- Cotton thread
- 1 round feather cushion pad (55cm/21½in in diameter)

from the toolbox

 top tip

Make sure the felt has some real wool content and isn't wholly synthetic.

1. Cut 1 x front piece from the front fabric and 2 x back pieces from the back fabric, using the templates on p.135.

If using dye/embroidery for the lion's face, transfer the design on p.135 onto the centre of the front piece (see p.11). Use the dye sticks first to colour-in (see p.12), then embroider the black lines on top. Either use the freehand-embroidery foot on your sewing machine and go back and forth along the lines (as if colouring-in with a pencil), or go over 3 or 4 times with a small, straight machine stitch.

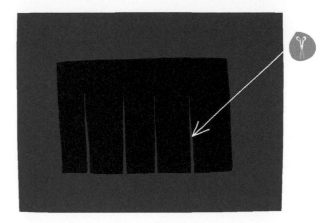

2. To make the mane, cut the felt into approximately 10 x 8cm/4 x 3in pieces, then, along the long side, cut 4 or 5 roughly 6cm/2½in vertical slits at regular intervals. This can be fairly imprecise as this gives a more 'natural' mane effect!

3. Starting around the face, build up the first layer of mane. Pin a length of mane to the front fabric, with the frilly cut edges facing towards the face. Stitch it on, about ½cm/¼in in from the uncut edge (you may need to slightly overlap and fold in the edges as you go to achieve a circular effect). Continue to build up the 'rounds' of mane pieces, moving outwards and slightly overlapping by about 1½cm/½in each time, leaving the cut bits to flow and flap freely. Continue until you have reached the edge. You'll need around 80–90 pieces in total.

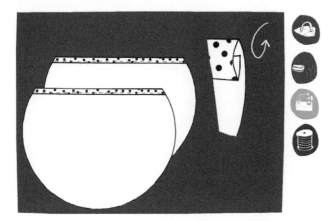

4. On each of the back pieces, turn in the straight edge ½cm/¼in to the wrong side. Press, then turn in a 1cm/½in hem and press again. Pin and stitch.

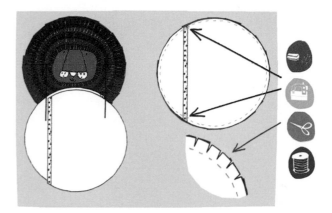

5. Overlap the back pieces, right side down, on top of the front 'felty-mane' piece, right side up. Pin in place. Stitch through both layers all the way around with a seam 1½cm/½in from the edge, back-stitching a few times on the bound edges of the back pieces for extra strength.

Trim any excess felt and clip the seam allowance all the way round being careful not to snip through the seam itself.

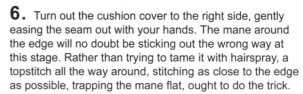

6. Turn out the cushion cover to the right side, gently easing the seam out with your hands. The mane around the edge will no doubt be sticking out the wrong way at this stage. Rather than trying to tame it with hairspray, a topstitch all the way around, stitching as close to the edge as possible, trapping the mane flat, ought to do the trick.

Insert the cushion pad, ruffle the mane and voilà!

hopscotch mat

To play a game of hopscotch with mini folk is one of life's best fun times. This one doubles-up as a picnic mat, garden lounger and all-round good number learning tool!

I used an old pillowcase and fabric dye sticks to create the numbers. I LOVE the 'coloured-in' effect the dye sticks give. Great to '' a slightly worn-out old pillowcase too!

from the toolbox

things you need

- Charcoal/black mid-weight cotton fabric (3m x 90cm/3yd x 36in)
- An old pillowcase or other white cotton fabric (50 x 75cm/20 x 30in)
- Fabric dye sticks
- Iron-on adhesive webbing (50 x 50cm/20 x 20in)
- Cotton thread

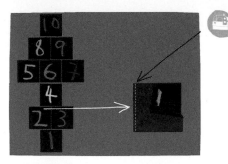

1. Cut out 10 squares, 30 x 30cm/12 x 12in, from the black cotton fabric. Keep the uncut cloth (180 x 90cm/72 x 36in) for backing the mat later.

Roughly cut 11 squares, 25 x 25cm/10 x 10in, from the white cotton fabric/pillowcase. Colour-in each piece with fabric dye sticks (ideally use 10 different colours and 2 pieces in the same colour for the number 10). Iron to fix. Back the squares with adhesive webbing.

2. Cut out your numbers (1–10) freehand. Iron the numbers in the centre of the pre-cut black squares to fuse (one number on each), and stitch round to secure, stitching as close to the edge as possible.

3. Lay your squares out on the floor in the correct positions and, row-by-row, place the numbers right-sides together, and stitch a 1cm/½in seam along the vertical edge. Stitch 2 to 3, 6 to 5 and 7, and 8 to 9. When you have finished all of the vertical seams, press them flat, re-lay on the floor and, with right sides together, row-by-row, stitch together each horizontal seam (1cm/½in). Press when complete.

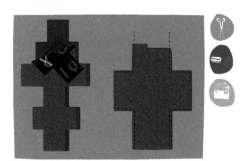

4. On the floor again, lay out as flat as possible the remaining piece of black cotton fabric, to cut the back of the mat. Lay the completed piece on top, right sides together, and cut round. Pin all around and stitch 3 edges together, leaving one of the small ends open, to turn out.

5. Clip and snip notches into all of the corners. Turn out.

Turn the open end in by 1cm/½in, press and stitch to close. With the mat flat (rhymes!), topstitch over each of the vertical and horizontal seams over the whole mat (as you would with a quilt).

Seek out a nice patch of grass and get hopping! If you like, you could paint some stones to use as markers, for a super rainbow effect.

gerald giraffe height chart

Measure your minis as they grow with Gerald the giraffe (and his nicely knitted roll-neck jumper). This is one to keep and a big improvement on pencil marks on the wall (which we used to do!). As it's not an item you will ever need to wash, biro works perfectly well on the cotton to mark down your measurements.

You can buy digitally printed fabric for this one (see details for buying on p.143), but if you are confident with a dye stick then you can hand-draw the giraffe using the template on p.135 as a guide.

things you need

- Printed Gerald fabric or piece of medium-weight cotton fabric with Gerald design drawn on (43 x 144cm/17 x 57in)
- Cotton thread
- Fabric dye sticks (if hand-drawing Gerald)
- 4 x wood strips (1½ x 8 x 43cm/½ x 3¼ x 17in)
- White paint and paint brush
- Hot glue gun and glue sticks
- Cotton webbing or good-quality string, for hanging strap (50cm/20in)
- T-shirt transfer paper
- Printer
- Ecru cotton fabric, for measurements (20 x 30cm/8 x 12in)

from the toolbox

top tip

Don't iron directly onto the 'transfer paper fabric', once made, as it will melt to the iron.

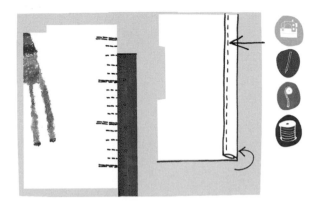

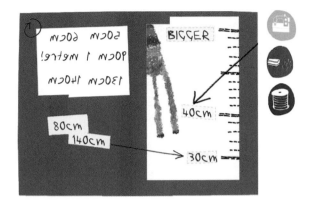

1. Along the long right-hand edge of your fabric, mark out measurements every 2cm/½in in pencil and embroider a 4cm/1½in line for each mark (I made every 10cm/4in mark thicker than the rest and 6cm/2½in long).

Turn in both long edges by ½cm/¼in, then turn in by ½cm/¼in again, press and stitch to hem.

2. Work out the measurements and words you'd like to include on your chart – I added my first measurement at 30cm/12in. Choose a font and type them up or scan your handwritten labels – remember that the text must be back-to-front before printing so that it will be the right way round when transferred. Remember to leave enough space around each label to make a fabric 'badge' you can attach to your chart. Print out your back-to-front measurements onto the T-shirt transfer paper. Transfer onto the ecru cotton fabric, following the instructions on the transfer paper pack.

Cut out each measurement and word badge from your transfer fabric. Pin each next to the relevant measurement mark and stitch all around to secure. Remember your measurements start at 30cm/12in, so you will need to make sure you site your chart at the right height from the floor when you hang it.

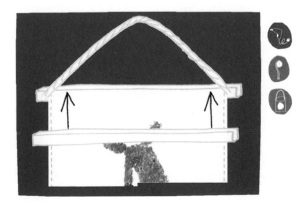

3. Paint the strips of wood white and leave to dry. Once dry, taking the first 2 strips of wood, hot glue the top raw edge of the height chart centrally onto one piece. Position the hanging strap, as shown, and hot glue this in place. Add another layer of hot glue and fix the second piece of wood on top, sandwiching the fabric and hanging strap in-between the 2 pieces. Repeat for the bottom of the height chart, omitting the strap. Once the glue has dried, hang the chart and measure your minis.

teepee

There is nothing better than hiding out in your very own teepee when you are little. This 'tenty-type' teepee accommodates numerous cuddly toys, a full-sized tea set, dinosaurs, knights, princesses, and even mum and dad at a push!

It's a whopper of a project size-wise, but not complicated to make. You'll feel a great sense of satisfaction when you've done it, and will have a nice place to sit and have a well-deserved cuppa too!

A medium-weight cotton canvas or cotton half panama will work well for this.

from the toolbox

things you need

- Main fabric – cotton canvas or half panama fabric (140cm x 4½m/55in x 5yd)
- Ties – cotton poplin or same as main fabric (40 x 24cm/16 x 10in)
- Cotton thread
- 4 x dowels (2½cm/1in diameter x 180cm/2yd)
- Rope, to secure the dowels

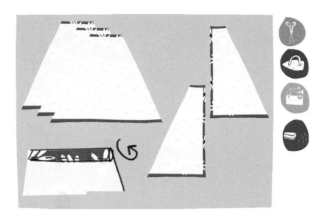

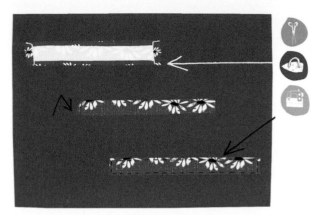

1. Using the templates on p.136, cut 3 x side panels from the main fabric. Then, fold the remaining fabric in half and cut 2 x front panels in one go.

On the side panels, turn the top and bottom edges over to the wrong side by 1cm/½in. Press. Turn over by 1cm/½in again. Press, pin and stitch.

On the front panels turn the top, bottom and right-angled edges over to the wrong side by 1cm/½in. Press. Turn over by 1cm/½in again. Press, pin and stitch.

2. Cut 4 pieces from the cotton poplin for the ties, 40 x 6cm/16 x 2½in. Turn over to the wrong side on all 4 edges by 1cm/½in, press. Fold in half lengthways and press. Stitch all around, as close to the edge as possible. Repeat for all the ties. Set aside.

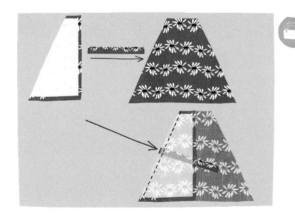

3. Starting with one of the front panels and one of the side panels, with right sides together, pin the seam on the long side. Slot in the first tie, 60cm/24in from the base, so it will stick out to the right side (outside) of the teepee. Stitch a 1cm/½in seam, securing the tie in place as you do. Strengthen the tie and each end of the seams by back-stitching a few times.

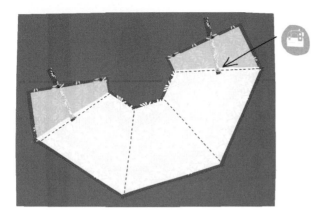

4. In the same manner, attach the other long side of the first side panel to the long side of the second side panel, then continue with the third side panel. Then attach the remaining front panel, remembering, when you pin the seam, to add in the second tie (60cm/24in from the base, as before). Press the seams.

5. Overlap the front panels by 1cm/½in and stitch to join the top 20cm/8in, strengthening each end of the join by back-stitching a number of times.

3½cm/1½in

6. To create the channels for the dowels, with wrong sides together, folding along each of the 4 main seams in turn, stitch a 3½cm/1½in seam along the full length of each seam, adding in the remaining 2 ties as you go. These should be slotted in directly opposite the other 2 ties, but this time they will stick out inside the teepee. Feed them up in-between the wrong sides of fabric and align them with where you can see the other ties sticking out. Make sure when seaming you stitch through all the layers of fabric and ties.

All you need to do now is slot the dowel rods into the channels, secure them together at the top with rope and a good knot, and get camping!

cardboard-roll zoo

A combo of cardboard rolls is great for this project, to give a variety of sizes. You'll need to help your little monkeys to cut, fold and slot the pieces together.

You will need

Variety of cardboard kitchen-paper rolls and toilet rolls

Scissors

Coloured paints

Paint brushes

ELEPHANT

Say hello to the circus with this clever elephant balancing on a stand. You need 1 toilet roll for the stand and 1 larger kitchen roll for the elephant.

1. Cut a 3cm/1¼in piece from the smaller roll.

2. Fold the larger roll flat and cut out an elephant shape, roughly following the diagram here. Be careful to leave the top of the ears attached.

3. Where you have cut the feet, fold the section in-between the feet to the inside of the elephant. Squish the roll a bit to round it out and stick the ears out a bit.

4. Paint the stand and the elephant, adding eyes and tusks. Leave to dry.

5. Slot the elephant onto the stand. Trunks away!

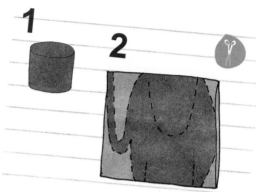

ZEBRA

You'll need 2 cardboard rolls for this happy chap.

1. Cut leg shapes into back and front of the first roll and poke them out a little bit.

2. Cut 2 ear shapes into the second roll and fold them up. Cut a slit halfway into the roll underneath the ears so the head roll will slot onto the leg roll. Fold in the mouth on head piece.

3. Paint your zebra all over with stripes, adding eyes, nostrils and hooves, and leave to dry. Slot together once dry.

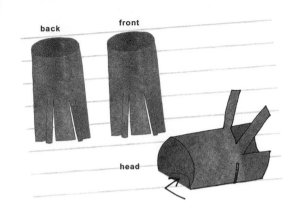

back   front

head

CROCODILE

You'll need 5 toilet rolls for snappy results!

1. On roll 1, cut 2 slits for the mouth and fold in the cut edges to make a pointy mouth. On rolls 2 and 3, cut 2 slits, 2cm/¾in long, on either side in the middle(ish), making sure they are opposite each other.

2. On roll 4, cut a tail shape. Next cut 2 strips for feet on roll 5, just under 2cm/¾ in wide, then cut claws at the end of each foot. Slot the foot pieces into the slits on rolls 2 and 3. Slot head roll into roll 2, then slot rolls 2 and 3 together. Slot tail into the other end of roll 3.

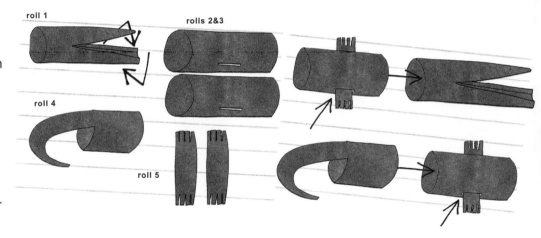

roll 1   rolls 2&3

roll 4

roll 5

3. Paint your crocodile green all over, then add eyes, teeth and scales. Leave to dry.

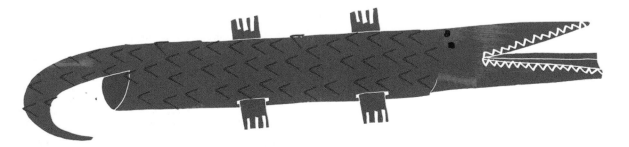

little helpers

Many of the templates can be photocopied directly from the book – simply enlarge at the percentage specified.

You will need to draw some of the templates to the correct scale using the grids provided as a guide. The dimensions of each square is specified next to each grid, and we've also included key length and width measurements to help you on your way.

Go to www.pavilionbooks.com/makesforminifolk to download and print full-size templates and printable grid guides.

top tip
Always check the grid scale or enlargement percentage before you begin as they vary.

templates

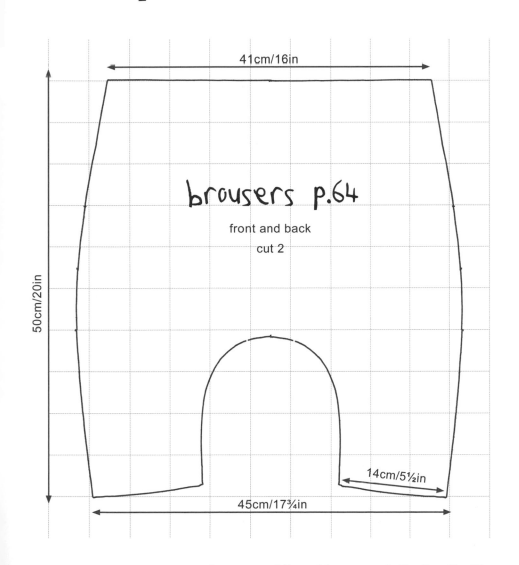

brousers p.64

front and back

cut 2

41cm/16in

50cm/20in

14cm/5½in

45cm/17¾in

brilliant bib p.16

enlarge by 400%

cut 1 x outer

cut 1 x lining

each square of the grid represents 5 x 5cm/2 x 2in

groceries p.80

dressing-up hats p.88

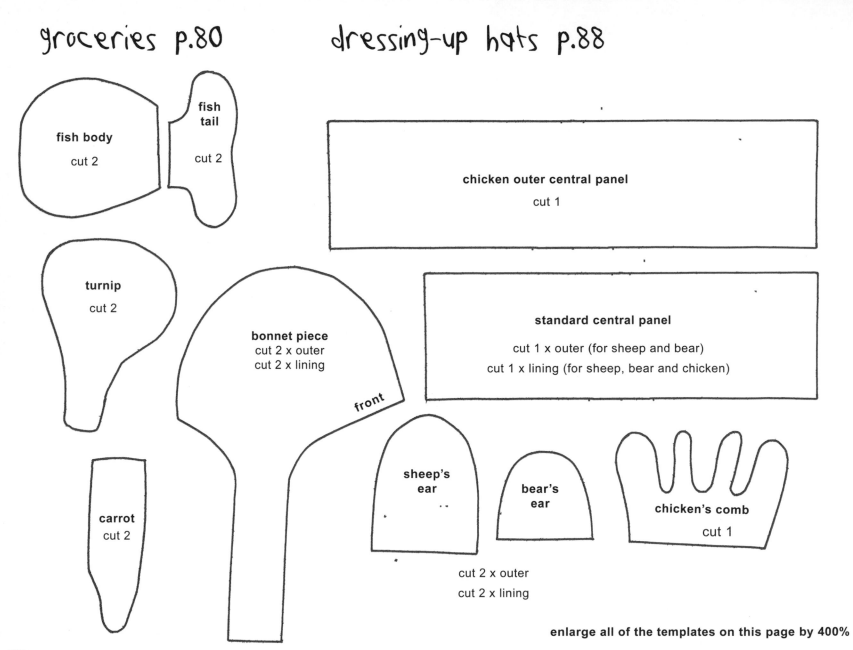

fish body

cut 2

fish tail

cut 2

chicken outer central panel

cut 1

turnip

cut 2

bonnet piece
cut 2 x outer
cut 2 x lining

front

standard central panel

cut 1 x outer (for sheep and bear)

cut 1 x lining (for sheep, bear and chicken)

sheep's ear

bear's ear

chicken's comb

cut 1

carrot
cut 2

cut 2 x outer

cut 2 x lining

enlarge all of the templates on this page by 400%

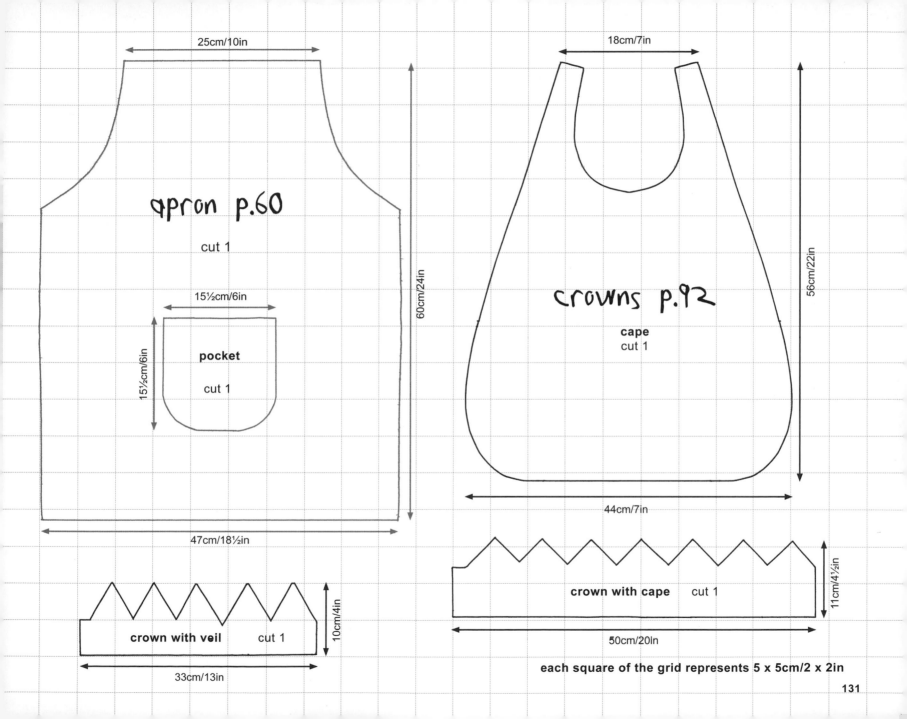

25cm/10in

apron p.60

cut 1

60cm/24in

15½cm/6in

15½cm/6in

pocket

cut 1

47cm/18½in

18cm/7in

crowns p.92

cape
cut 1

56cm/22in

44cm/7in

crown with veil   cut 1

10cm/4in

33cm/13in

crown with cape   cut 1

11cm/4½in

50cm/20in

each square of the grid represents 5 x 5cm/2 x 2in

mobile p.31

enlarge by 200%

cut 1 of each

tree

tree & leaves

car

wheels

bird

mushroom

spots for mushroom

rainbow

house

door

sheep

embroidered cushion p.34

enlarge by 200%

overalls p.70

each square of the grid represents 10 x 10cm/4 x 4in

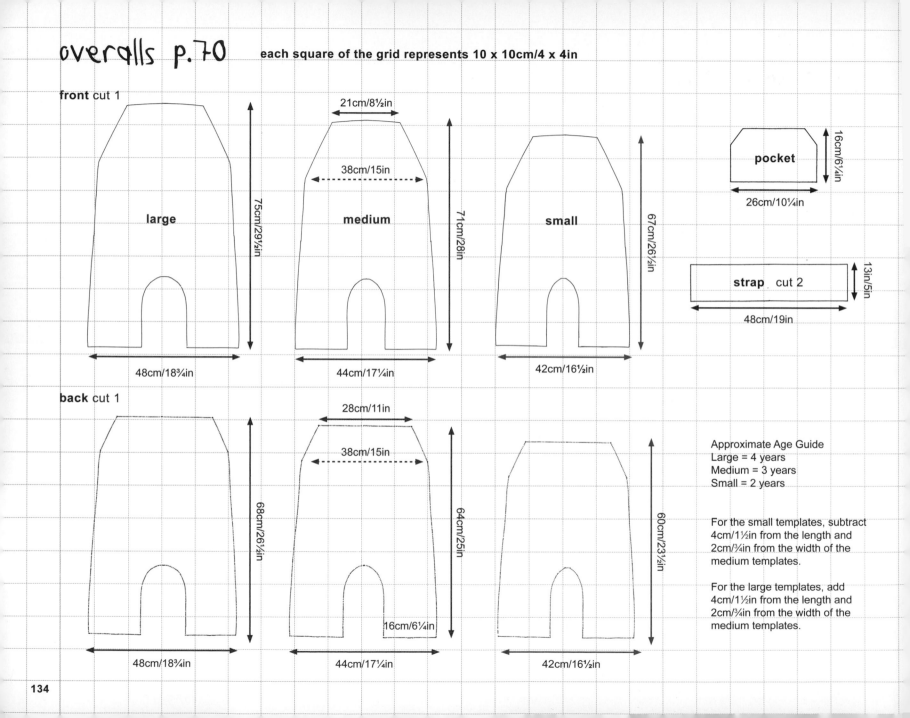

front cut 1

large — 75cm/29½in — 48cm/18¾in

medium — 21cm/8½in — 38cm/15in — 71cm/28in — 44cm/17¼in

small — 67cm/26½in — 42cm/16½in

pocket — 16cm/6¼in — 26cm/10¼in

strap cut 2 — 13in/5in — 48cm/19in

back cut 1

large — 68cm/26½in — 48cm/18¾in

medium — 28cm/11in — 38cm/15in — 64cm/25in — 16cm/6¼in — 44cm/17¼in

small — 60cm/23½in — 42cm/16½in

Approximate Age Guide
Large = 4 years
Medium = 3 years
Small = 2 years

For the small templates, subtract 4cm/1½in from the length and 2cm/¾in from the width of the medium templates.

For the large templates, add 4cm/1½in from the length and 2cm/¾in from the width of the medium templates.

lion cushion p.112

To make this template...
attach a piece of string to a pencil. Measure the
length of string to 28cm/11in – the radius of the
circle. With one hand, hold the end of the string
in the centre of a sheet of paper and with the
other hand pull the string tight, then draw round
to create a full circle. Cut out this paper pattern
then use it as template to cut out 1 front piece of
fabric and 2 back pieces.

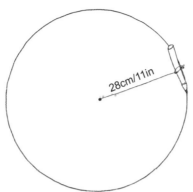

28cm/11in

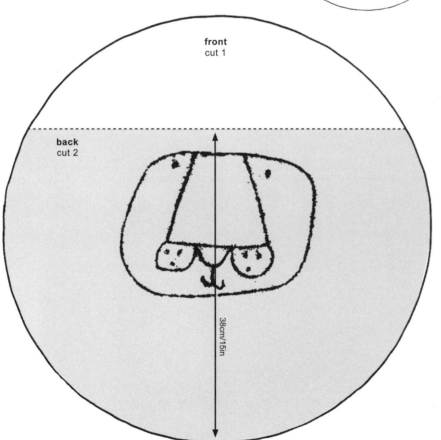

front
cut 1

back
cut 2

38cm/15in

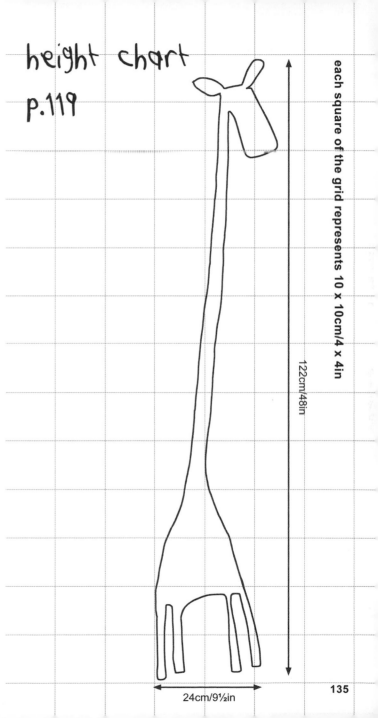

height chart
p.119

each square of the grid represents 10 x 10cm/4 x 4in

122cm/48in

24cm/9½in

135

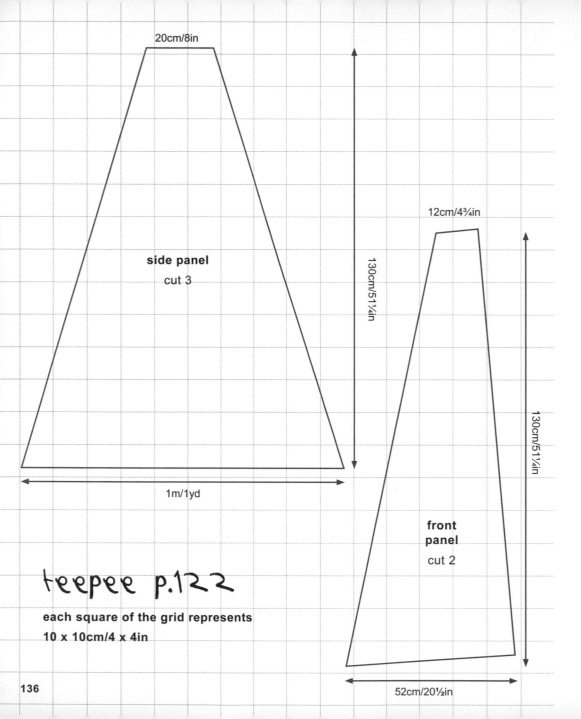

20cm/8in

side panel

cut 3

130cm/51¼in

1m/1yd

12cm/4¾in

front panel

cut 2

130cm/51¼in

52cm/20½in

teepee p.122

each square of the grid represents
10 x 10cm/4 x 4in

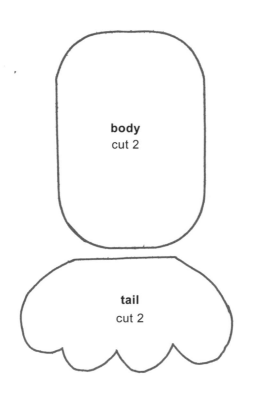

fish pencil case p.48

enlarge by 400%

body

cut 2

tail

cut 2

long-legged nell p.18

each square of the grid represents 5 x 5cm/2 x 2in

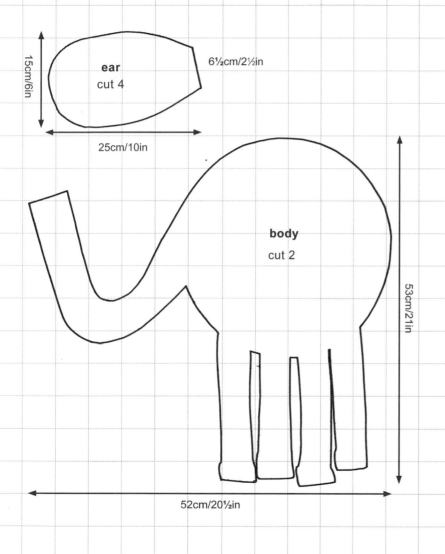

15cm/6in

ear
cut 4

6½cm/2½in

25cm/10in

body
cut 2

53cm/21in

52cm/20½in

hobby horse p.104

enlarge by 400%

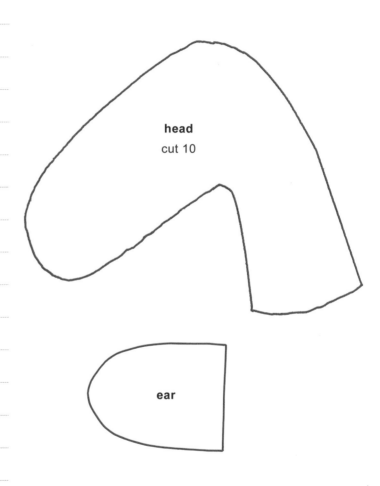

head
cut 10

ear

bendable book p.20

The templates for the bendable book are to scale and can be photocopied directly from the book

rainbow

cut 1 of each

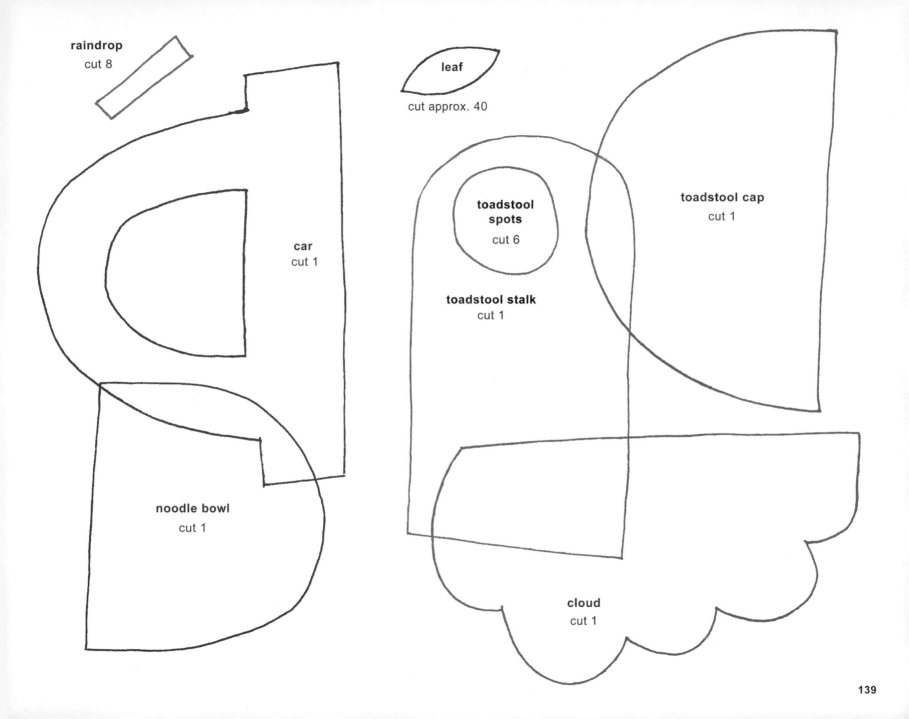

raindrop
cut 8

leaf
cut approx. 40

car
cut 1

toadstool cap
cut 1

toadstool spots
cut 6

toadstool stalk
cut 1

noodle bowl
cut 1

cloud
cut 1

139

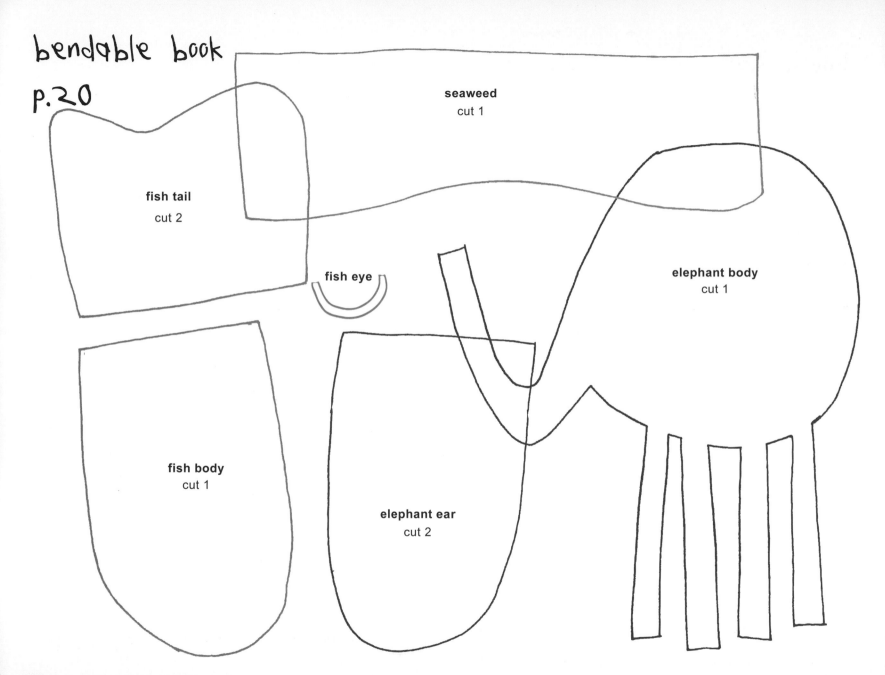

bendable book
p.20

seaweed
cut 1

fish tail
cut 2

fish eye

elephant body
cut 1

fish body
cut 1

elephant ear
cut 2

lunch bag p.54

handle   cut 2
30cm/12in
5cm/2in

main
cut 1
20cm/8in
12cm/4¾in
46cm/18in

side panel
cut 2
20cm/8in
10cm/4in

baby-changing pouch p.50

31cm/12¼in

cut 4 x outer

cut 4 x lining

24cm/9½in

34½cm/13½in

romper p.66

41cm/16¼in

body
cut 2 x outer
cut 2 x lining

28cm/11in

45½cm/18in

40½cm/16in

42cm/16½in

10cm/4in

strap   cut 2 x outer fabric
30cm/12in
4cm/1½in

each square of the grid represents 5 x 5cm/2 x 2in

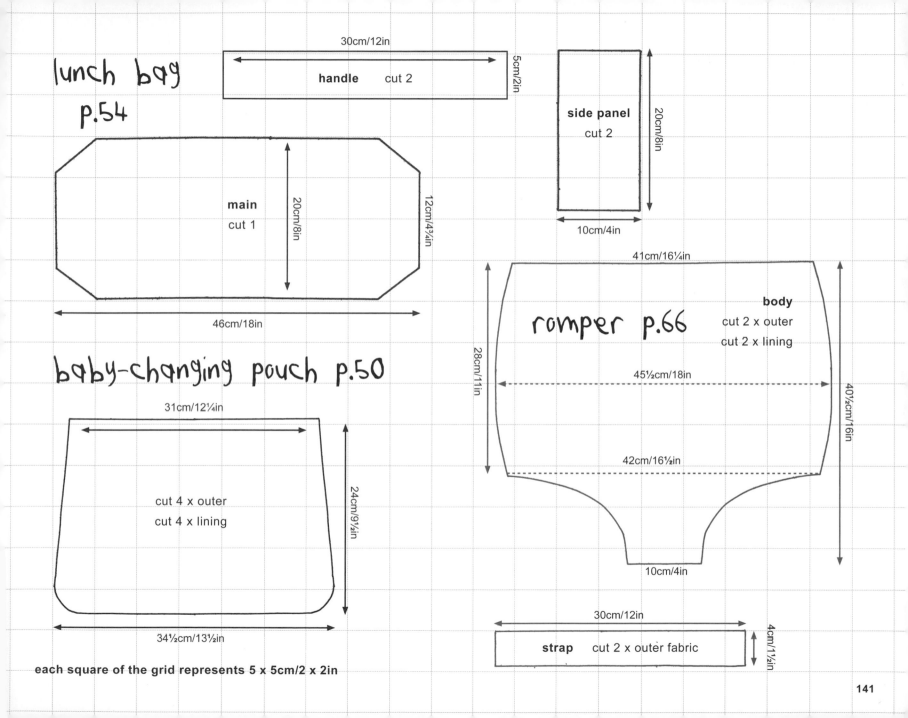

sleepsack p.37

each square of the grid represents 5 x 5cm/2 x 2in

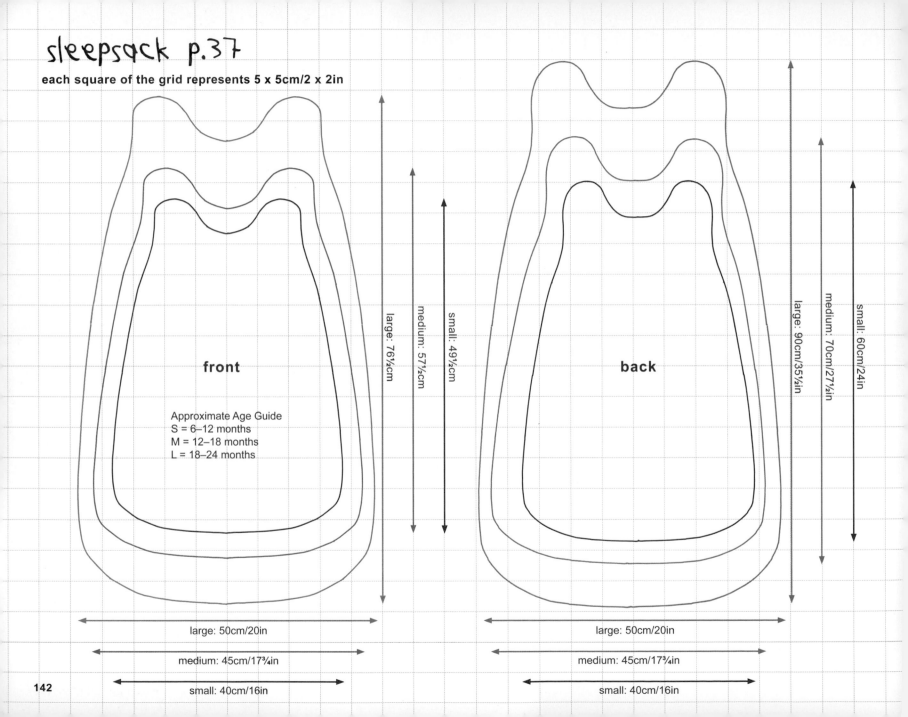

front

Approximate Age Guide
S = 6–12 months
M = 12–18 months
L = 18–24 months

back

large: 76½cm

medium: 57½cm

small: 49½cm

large: 90cm/35½in

medium: 70cm/27½in

small: 60cm/24in

large: 50cm/20in

medium: 45cm/17¾in

small: 40cm/16in

large: 50cm/20in

medium: 45cm/17¾in

small: 40cm/16in

resources

DIGITALLY PRINTED FABRIC

Woven monkey
www.wovenmonkey.co.uk
For small runs of digitally printed fabric, starting from 1m/1yd, this is the place to order fabric for the *Makes For Mini Folk* projects, available to buy directly from the website. See p.10 for more information.

SHOPS & SUPPLIERS (& FAVOURITE GO-TO PLACES) DIRECTORY

Amazon
So easy, I've been known to order things in my sleep. Online shopping becomes a bit of a godsend when you're in the early stages of baby life. And after that too actually! Again, a one-stop shop for pretty much anything and everything, and super for tools, sewing machines, bodkins, glue guns, thread, zips, cushion fillers, fabric crayons, paint sticks... Thank you to all the delivery folk out there! We 'heart' you!

The Cloth House
www.theclothhouse.com
For wonderful cottons, linens and silks.

The Cloth Shop
www.theclothshop.net
A great range of natural fabrics.

Colourful Felt
www.colourfulfelt.co.uk
Fabulous for felt!

Dylon
www.dylon.co.uk
For machine dyes.

eBay
A regular 'go-to' for almost anything and everything. Lots of new bits for sale these days, but still good for 'vintage' or 'old' fabrics, if popping out to scour the charity shops is a bit hectic with mini folk tagging along.

Fred Aldous
www.fredaldous.co.uk
Wonderful art and craft shops in Manchester and Leeds. Everything available online too. Great for glue guns, paper, haberdashery and more.

Ikea
(and other similar homeware shops)
www.ikea.com
Shops worldwide. GREAT for collecting LARGE discarded cardboard boxes, usually in pretty good condition too! Go with an empty car boot to stock up.

Janome
www. janome.co.uk
For sewing machines and other sewing supplies.

John Lewis
www.johnlewis.com
For fabrics, haberdashery goods and a wide range of sewing machines.

Merchant & Mills
www.merchantandmills.com
A favourite for WONDERFUL linens and dreamy denims (perfect for making Long-Legged Nell). And some pretty fantastic 'grown-up' dress patterns of their own, if you fancy making something for yourself.

Merrick & Day
www.merrick-day.com
For great-quality cushion fillers.

Nova Trimmings
www.novatrimmingsltd.co.uk
For zips and trimmings.

Ray Stitch
www.raystitch.co.uk
I came across these guys by accident, and I am so pleased I did. A beautifully edited range of fabrics and, as it says on their strapline 'a one-stop sewing shop'! Perfect for organic fleece for the sleep sack and a winter version of the romper and overalls too.

keep in touch

If you would like to keep in touch and see what's happening in my world, have a look at: www.lisastickleystudio.com

I'm also on...
Instagram @lisastickley_studio
Pinterest @lisastickley_studio
Twitter @lisastickley_

So why not say a 'social-media hello'?

I'd love to hear from you.

Lisa x

A big thank you

Some fab folk have helped me make this book possible. I'd like to say a HUGE thank you to all of them.

Katie Cowan, for believing in the mini acorn from which this book has grown (and for her unwavering love of dungarees). Krissy Mallett, for being super supportive throughout the whole project, quietly and expertly keeping me in check and helping me bring the jumble of ideas I had in my head to life on paper. Emily Preece-Morrison for her superb editing skills and Amy Christian for her crafty know-how. Michelle Mac, for her expertise with layouts, letters and listening to what I was after on each and every page, and Sophie Yamamoto for her excellent design work.

Polly Powell, for her perpetually cheery encouragement, for putting together the great team at Pavilion and for giving me a much-needed leg-up into the world of writing, illustrating and making books a few years ago. Thank you Polly.

Neil Dunnicliffe, for being a super chap, excellent editor and holding my hand from the very beginning of my literary journey into all things mini.

Colette Whitehouse, Catherine Ward and Frida Green for helping me spread the word about my books, putting up with my pre-book-fest nerves (!) and for their general super promo skills.

Jodie Hodges, Emily Talbot and Molly Jamieson at United Agents, for being all-round wondrous. Thank you for looking after me and welcoming me into the fold!

My dream team: stylist and photographer, Katie Frade and Ben Anders, for skilfully bringing everything to life in pictures. It's great to be back in the saddle again and I can't think of anyone I'd rather have worked with on my first big 'new chapter' project than these two fab people.

A big thank you to Vanessa Leigh-Anders for providing such a wonderful space to shoot in and very yummy cake! And a VERY special thank you to Alfie Leigh-Anders for all of his doodles, modelling moments and general super cute, squishy-squashy, mini wondrousness!

To Mum, Dad, Sally, Glyn, Anna, Hayden, Henry, Hannah, Vito, Jo, Vix, Farah and Katie, thank you for always being there, especially when things get tough. I couldn't do any of this without your encouragement and support, AND (for the former folk) supa-dupa grandparent babysitting assistance too!

To Richard, the best, most grounded, supportive husband and super daddy the girls and I could wish for. Thank you for holding my hand through thick and thin. To Edith and Ada, my magically marvellous mini ones, without whom none of this would exist. You make me smile and laugh every day and are an inspiration in everything I do. Love you so much I might burst!